THE LAST TRAVEL
Hmong exile stories

By the same author
"Tougain, the lazy man"
"The little boy with the Halloween basket"

Maiv Lis

THE LAST TRAVEL
Hmong exile stories

Cover : Mélodie Sidoti

© 2025 "The Intellectual Property Code prohibits copies or reproductions intended for collective use. Any representation or reproduction, in whole or in part, made by any process whatsoever, without the consent of the author or his successors in title, is unlawful and constitutes an infringement, under the terms of Articles L.335-2 et seq. of the Intellectual Property Code."

To my mother,
and to all the women who make this world a sweeter place.

Introduction

"The last travel" is a testimonial book telling the journey that led the Hmong into exile, at the end of the Vietnam War, with no hope of return.

It is a story told in two voices: the first part is my mother's, and the second part, mine. I wanted to show that each person, while living the same experience, can have a different point of view of the same situation.

In addition, this book evokes the travel from one place to another and the Great Journey of life, which begins with birth and ends with death.

May this book bring you home, taking the time to be with your beloved family. Nothing is more precious than having a "sweet home," the source of every human being. Because, despite our differences, one must never forget that for each thing, there is always a beginning and an end.

Talking about Mao

My mother recorded her life story on an audio cassette on July 11, 1997. How seventy-seven years could last a forty-five-minute recording? Today, four years after she left us, in 2012, it feels like yesterday. Now is the time to finish my mourning, or to really start it. I put the tape in the player: first I shivered. I recognize her voice I thought I have forgotten. But, it is real, now she has really left us. Then the reality throws me to the sadness I did not want to accept until now. My heart wants to leave my chest, and my tears flow like a river.

I imagine her in her room, in front of the little radio cassette she gave my sister, which I now use to listen to her.

I hear her needle running through the white fabric, where she places her cross stitches. She creates an embroidery. The thread sings when she pulls it over her shoulder! What color is this thread? There are red, green and blue, I can see. Her favorite colors.

Some of these linen threads, lost under the sofa, sometimes come out still now.

A slight deviation in her voice, followed by a little click, makes me understand that she is wetting another thread.

She continues telling without pause. It is her life she knows by heart. And her remembrance are still good.

On my little computer, I instantly translate her words. I paste and gather the pieces of memories, sometimes full of inconsistencies. I feel sad not have done this translation when she was alive. I could ask her questions, get more details... Maybe I thought she never dies.

She says she is like a "mother bird". It is true, I think. Her life is a labor life, since her birth in a family of Hmong farmers in Laos.

She never stops working because her target was the survival of her family.

In this transcription, I tried to be closest with her talk which is sometimes incoherents (dates, locations, history people...). During your read, do not forget that it is her point of view.

Let us follow her in her "mother bird" life.

Mao
Like a mother bird

1

I was born in Laos and my life is already destined for a life of labor, like many Hmong girls in my village. Since the dawn of time, I have believed that women are only born to experience this destiny of labor. Thus, our mothers, and before them, our mothers' mothers have all plowed the lands of our ancestors...

During years of marriage, my parents were unable to have children. It is very bad within the Hmong community: a childless couple is supposed to not have done good things in their previous life. My mother begins treatment for sterility by using plants. She gives birth to my brother Tcha.

Three years later, still thanks to the treatment, I am born. My parents named me Mao, but as I am in fragile health, my parents think that this name does not suit me. So they decide to ask a woman from the Heu clan to "rename" me. It is a common practice to be baptized by someone of one's choice, which often brings good luck. Since then, I have been called Mao Heu. But on papers, I bear my father's name. He is from the Xiong clan.

We live in a busy village in the Hmong mountains

called *Teb nyub qus*[1]. My parents are farmers; they grow rice. Before the sun rises and the rooster crows, under the last rays of the moon, my parents are already up. Whilst my mother is busy preparing the morning meal and feeding the animals, my father cleans the last tools: spades, scythes, knife blades serrated and worn by rust...

He shakes the baskets outside and touches up the parts untied by use. Then they go to the fields, and we don't see them again until very late in the evening. Despite their absences, my brother and I do not complain. It is normal, and we do not know we miss them.

Some neighbors stay in the village to take care of the farm tasks: feeding the animals, preparing meals, looking after the youngest children... like my brother and me.

Life in the village is tough, but fortunately, everyone is helpfull. Some women even allow other children to come and suckle their breasts, when their mothers are busy, or when they cannot have enough milk.

I am often very hungry, and when one day, the "aunt[2]" who is looking after me offers me her milk, I throw myself on her breasts and suckle greedily before going to hide shamely. I am also envious when I see others eating; and even when it is not food, my imagination makes me believe that there is rice in the

---

[1] Teb nyub qus, a famous place known as Moutain of buffle.
[2] We usually call adults "aunt" or "uncle", out of restpect and to avoid explaining complicated family relationships.

bamboo transported by uncles coming from Paksé. It is true that the freshly cut bamboo gives off a scent of fresh rice from the fire...

My parents feel sorry for me. They whish to be able to feed us every day, but despite their work, they cannot provide for our needs, and we spend our time moving. They want to find a field that produces enough rice where we can settle permanently. Whether from Phao-Khao to Long-Cheng or from Te-Nyu-Cru to Phu-Mou, we travel through these different villages several times in our lives but cannot find a place that can welcome us for good.

Fortunately, they never give up and try slash-and-burn farming. They channel the fire into huge squares of land that burn to serve as fertilizer. But the weeds on the high ground are too damp. The only way is to cut them and make small piles before burning them: a few rice plants grow slightly here and there.

The fields are a day's walk away, in a place where it is hard to settle alone. In these mountains, you must be surrounded by other groups to survive. In addition, the topography of the place do not allow for solid housing construction.

After the harvest, my parents load several bags of rice onto the backs of sturdy horses to bring them back to the village. The return is fraught with pitfalls: the humidity and rain make the roads muddy and slippery. Of course, while working on their fields day after day, the weeds have had time to grow, and nature has taken over, making each trip back very difficult.

Exhausted by the round trips, they stayed several

days in the village for housework, and the rice stock quickly sells out.

We often go hungry for two or three years before the land is warm enough to grow crops. Otherwise, we eat whatever is available: roots or tree bark that my parents cleverly turn into flour. To do this, trees on the hillside must be cut down and dragged to accessible places; women and children cut them up and bring them home. Then, we remove the bark and cut the trunk into strips that must be dried over the fire or in the sun during the day.

Once dry, the strips are crumbled, put into bags, and sieved for hours. The powder is collected, then water is added and mixed without stopping to allow the flour to clump together at the bottom of the container. We slowly remove the water, and finally, a small quantity of flour is collected, like a precious treasure that we dry near the ashes. It is mixed with rice or semolina to make it more consistent and better. It is often the only meal of the day.

My brother and I have a hard time growing properly: our bellies are often swollen, and our bronchial tubes are congested. Our bones become fragile, our lips are white, and our cheeks are pale.

In these living conditions, infant mortality is high, and my parents try to have as many children as possible. My mother begins another treatment for sterility. She gives birth to a boy who dies at the age of nine months. In the countryside, we are very superstitious. When something terrible happens, it is often a sign of bad luck, which can either mean that we did something horrible in our previous life, or that someone has cast a spell on us...

I think he died of malnutrition: my mother does not have much breastmilk and works too much. Additionally, there are no hospitals, and many people only treat themselves with opium. It is the only remedy that quickly relieves pain. For the rest, we depend on the shaman. He is the one who cures all sickness. Despite this, my father, who is himself a shaman, often treats himself with opium, which does not prevent him from having pain all over his body.

Misfortunes never come alone, and during my little brother's funeral, many criticized my parents in all sorts of ways for the performance of this most difficult and painful funeral rite. Many stay awake to watch over the deceased for several days and nights. Known or unknown guests come to pay their respects, even if he was only a small baby. The grieving family must ensure that food is available on guests' tables. This is the solidarity among peasant farmers: if no one came to the funeral, it would mean that the family was not well appreciated.

People live day by day, and this kind of drama shows ambiguous and sometimes ruthless human relationships. Slanderous people say, "Since funerals are so strange, everyone can sleep with everyone or marry everyone in your clan[3]".

The difference in my father's clan is that the

---

3 Each Hmong family belongs to a clan. Within the same clan, practices may differ. Differences are generally frowned upon (deformities, illnesses, sterility...)..

deceased is laid down with his head against the pillar as if when sleeping. I do not understand this kind of critizes, but after the funeral, my father decides to take us to live with his family in Long-Cheng. Our survival has become less complicated with them, and my brother and I can finally grow as we become healthier. My brother even starts to flirt with girls.

It has been like this since the dawn of time. My brother will become a father and carry the weight of our family on his shoulders. At least, that is how it is in the Hmong family. The man bears the family's burden and must provide for their needs. At all costs, he must preserve the name of his ancestors and their honor.

I am prepared to become a good daughter-in-law, well-educated, well-obedient, and able to manage an entire household. As with many young people, it is the parents who arrange the marriages of their children, especially girls. Marriages with love are rare.

2

My parents rarely ask me for anything. As I am the only girl of the family, with a somewhat rebellious temper, my mother, after giving me her main educational tasks, lets me go about my business. A young man courts me but is penniless and does not dare ask for my hand. I find myself married to a son from a good family. The young man's name is Tou Lis, whose family lives a day's walk from my village.

Shortly before my wedding, I suddenly lose my voice due to a severe sore throat, and can only whisper my consent.

At seventeen, I become a wife[4] and leave my parents with a heavy heart. I know it is forever. You never return home when you leave your family to build your own.

As soon as I cross the door of my childhood house, my tears and my backward glances have no impact on the hearts of those who stole my adolescence and my family. Today, I become a stranger to everyone: to my own people and to the family I marry. Indeed, a Hmong girl does not marry only the man who will

---
4 See the *Getting married section* for a brief description of the marriage proposal ritual.

become the father of her children, but his entire family, including his lineage, his customs, and his traditions.

I find this situation unfair, but I am resigned since any protest is useless: it would be futile to fight and rebel. It would only harm my parents and those of her clan.

I obediently continue with the course of my life; my mother has diligently prepared me for it since I was very young. However, the separation is difficult, and it takes me days to get used to it. After three days[5], I resigned. I emerge from my silence and participate in my new life.

*

I soon discovered that my husband also obeys his parents by taking me as his wife. He has no feelings for me, or do not show it, and seems to accept me only to make his parents happy. Despite this, I am not well appreciated: I am not the obedient and submissive wife that a man of his clan deserves.

My husband comes from a very reputable family whose great-grandfather originates from China. My father-in-law is a man who owns a considerable family estate, inherited from his parents, with horses, buffaloes, pigs, and chickens. All the farm animals and the vast fields are part of this heritage, which is the pride of his clan. Everyone appreciates his family. There is always food at the table and an empty place

---

[5] Traditionally, the bride must stay in her room for three days and three nights.

for a surprise guest. It is an important practice for the reputation of the family.

My mother-in-law runs the house with prudence, watching over the treasure hoard amassed by the sweat of the housewives, who are both housekeepers at home and farmers in the fields. My sisters-in-law work steadily, from morning to night: weeding the fields from bottom to top, from top to bottom, feeding the animals, cooking for the whole family, made up of brothers-in-law, sisters-in-law, aunts, uncles,… With enough food only to fill their stomach as a reward, it is considered an unspeakable luxury. Not a single soap, not a jewel, or new piece of clothing, except for the New Year party. It is only during this time that the girls show themselves in pretty embroidered costumes, in bright colors, in the hope of finding a rich husband whom they could serve with the same enthusiasm as at home…

As always, no complaints come to scratch about this education that seems natural, and the idea does not occur to them that another way of doing things could exist.

I immediately immerse myself in their lives, like throwing a sponge into water. You must absorb the remarks, the orders, and the educational shock. There is plenty to do, and I contribute primarily to the household chores and fieldwork.

A year after my marriage, I give birth to my first child: a boy, named Guia. After cutting down the trees and plowing the farmland, I fall seriously ill. With hollow cheeks and completely lethargic, I owe my recovery only to a message sent to my parents, who come running with chickens and pigs to feed me. I happily notice the presence of my parents remaining in my life. They take care of me until my recovery.

Childbirths follow one after another almost every year. And as with every birth, Tou is missing, I do not note children's dates of birth. I do not read or write.

*

The rice and corn fields are close to our house. They are so vast that if a gunshot fires from one side, it cannot be heard from the other side. Now, I live like the labor of my parents.

It is as if history was repeating itself endlessly: weeding, harvesting, picking up bundles of rice to thresh them, separating the grains from the branches, pounding them, removing the husks, storing them in bags... Surrounded by all my children, who are all very young (one clinging to my legs, one stuck to my stomach, and one on my back), I am not exempted from work, even from the most challenging task. In contrast, my numerous children are detrimental to my availability, compared to my other daughters-in-law, who have few children and do no more than me.

Having children is a big handicap, while not having any is a curse and allows the husband the right to go and take other wives. However, I defend myself with my strong personality, and Tou has never been able to take another wife.

During my pregnancy, pounding rice remains one of the most exhausting tasks: after having beaten the bundles of rice with all my strength with the help of a large pestle, I had to collect the grains still covered with their husks to put them in the mortar. The mortar is made of a large wooden container; the pestle is attached to a large cleat with a footrest. I have to press on the footrest with all my strength so that the pestle removes the husks by crushing itself on the rice placed in the container. I feel my belly swelling as if it is about to burst after working on this task for half my day.

It goes on for years until the day my father-in-law makes a pestle that works with water. Now, all that remains to monitor the work that drags on into the night. This hydraulic pestle allows me to crush a basket of ten bundles, and if I get up early, I can do a little more before going to the fields. It is a victory when that is the case, but the night is short and the day even longer, which does not end when I return from the fields. I have to cook and clean the tools to prepare for the next day's work. There is no rest, only a few hours of sleep during the night.

In the morning, at the first crowing of the rooster, I have to get up to go and get water from the river. I have to bring back five buckets of water from the river, huge and heavy buckets, which I cannot carry fully on my back. I have to be clever because you have to be smart to survive: I fill the bucket halfway, which I then put on my back, and then, using a small basin, I top off the bucket until it reaches a weight I can carry. It has to be full to avoid having to come back too often. Then, it is with an extraordinary effort, one knee on the ground, that I straighten up, screaming to free my aching body from this burden, that must represent much more than my weight. The water is used to cook, give to animals, and allow some to wash themselves...

I prepare a large pot of rice, which is so heavy that it takes two people to lift it. When the meal is ready, I can rarely sit down with everyone. With my children of all ages, I must first feed them to calm them down as they often gnaw at hunger. When I finally sit down, there is no more broth to eat with the rest of the rice: sometimes, I even have to scrape the bottom of the chili pestle to season the rice balls that I am still lucky enough to recover from the bottom of the pot.

During the day, towards the end of my pregnancy, when I am useless in the fields, I stay in the village to do daily chores.

I feed the animals; the fat of the oldest pigs is used for cooking food, and the youngest are slaughtered for their meat. When we sacrifice a pig, the entire village is invited. It is common for a party to be held with all the neighbors and friends. If some people does not come, it is because they are angry, and if there are few people, it is because the family is not appreciated and will not be invited if an opportunity arises elsewhere...

I can have some leftover meat during these holidays, but I rarely have the right to chicken meat. There is too little, and I can always and only contend with broth. During these moments, I feel very lonely and often hide to cry silently over my fate. No matter a daughter-in-law's feelings, there is no room for joy, laughter, only tears...

It is hard to make a place for yourself in a family other than the one you were born in. I know that no matter what I do, I will always be considered a stranger. The stranger, doomed to solitude, must not complain.

*

After my eighth child, my mother-in-law make it clear to Tou that there are too many mouths to feed. The children are still very young, but after cutting down the trees, mowing, and plowing the fields, my husband and I are invited to go and build a house in Long-Cheng.

It is a blessing in disguise since my parents live in this town, and I can finally live with my family again. I can relax my nerves without feeling judged for what I do or do not do. Without my husband's family pressure, I feel better, and the children can grow up peacefully. My eldest children begin to help me, and I finally see the purpose of my life as a woman: to feed my children, like a mother bird, tirelessly.

Yes, I feel like a "mother bird". Always in an everlasting search, from morning to night, to bring back something to feed my little "sparrows". I use all my ideas by putting all the means to provide for their daily needs.

I grow vegetables to sell them on the market. I harvest vines that I dry... My work allows me to have enough to exchange for salt, oil, or rice so that everyone can grow up properly: you must not believe that everyone knows how to grow up alone, no matter how much their parents love them. You must never think like that. Being a mother means doing everything, no matter the price or how hungry and tired you are...

To help the children grow up, I feed them semolina for years.

My father-in-law has money to buy rice, which he leaves for his other son, whose wife is disabled and with whom he lives.

There are too many of us. People may be afraid of us, that we may ask for help. But I have never thought of begging. My role as a mother is to find something to feed my little ones.

3

My parents-in-law seize every opportunity and start growing opium, which they sold to Laotians and neighboring countries. It helps them earn a good living.

Tou and I try our best to provide for our family, but I find it unfair to receive no help from my in-laws. Fortunately, my parents set an example for me, and I follow in their footsteps. I continue to work hard in the fields with the help of my eldest daughters.

When the war starts, Vang Pao[6], a Hmong who works for the Americans, begins to enlist men to fight against the Pathet Lao. All this is beyond us because we are simply peasants trying to survive daily. But my parents-in-law like honor and encourage Tou to join the American army. I am totally against this idea: who will help me in the fields, with so many children who do not leave my side for even a second?

My mother-in-law decides to ask the spirits for their

---

6 Vang Pao (1929-2011): Laotian general and warlord who commanded a CIA-backed "secret army" of Hmong guerrillas. Considered a traitor to his country by Communist Laos, he died in exile in the USA, having fought all his life in vain for the return of the Hmong people to Laos.

opinion. She sacrifices a chicken, which indicates by its turned-up legs that her son should not enlist. But she disagrees this conclusion.

"It's because you don't want him to leave!"

She accuses me of turning the chicken's legs upside down.

As she is tenacious and is used to getting what she wants, she sacrifices a second chicken. She plucks it, guts it, cooks it and finally reads from the chicken's stiff, straight legs that the spirits are in favor of her son's enlistment.

From this point on, Tou has been constantly away while I continue my work with my sisters-in-law, between fields, household chores, and maternity... When he returns, he is never alone. As a senior officer, he is accompanied by his soldiers. It is an occasion to kill a cow to celebrate his return, considered a miracle because many men never return.

One day, following a hearty meal offered by my parents-in-law, we learn that the enemy is en route to hunt down the resistance fighters. The men start to flee.

The Viet Cong believe that Vang Pao's soldiers have taken the path to the fields and pursue them there. But there were only a few children and a few women busy harvesting.

My children and I are in the house when we hear shooting.

We hear someone shout, "Get down!" and instinctively, we throw ourselves to the ground without thinking. Bullets whistle above our heads, all around us, and we believe this is our last moment. Afterward, someone else shouts and orders us to run away. Fear in our stomachs, we rush towards the door mindlessly, in total panic. Outside, there is blood everywhere. We do not know who is hit or who this blood belongs to, and we tremble with fear.

A little further on, we meet a relative, and unfortunately, we understand that it is the one who has been injured. "It's you; it's your blood!" He replies, "Yes, it's me; I'm hit." That is all. We continue on our way, running, without thinking of helping him, wheareas he staggers away in another direction. In any case, we will surely be dead soon, as well. While we run across a steep field to escape, we see the faces of the enemy turned towards us on the other side. The corn has reached knee height. We do not have time to avoid them and stamp on them, our hearts heavy at having to destroy the fruit of our labor.

We are helpless, lost, drained, our heads and minds clouded by fear and incomprehension of this nightmare. As a precaution, before leaving the house, I managed to grab a few lamps and a few bottles of oil that I carry in my belt made of tissue.

Accompanied by two of my sons and two of my eldest daughters, we fumble around to avoid being spotted, then, I light a lamp when we are far enough away, and it is completely dark. Our elders routinely say: "At night, the eyes are blinded by ashes." Yes, no matter how much we open our eyes, we see nothing, absolutely nothing. The darkness is total. After crossing a road, we reach a plateau; raindrops begin to fall in places. When we light the lamps, we discover that they are droplets falling from the trees: they sparkle on the leaves. The ground is reddish; no wonder, it is the color of the earth here. The creatures of the night chat happily.

I am carrying my daughter Zeu. Choua, my eldest daughter, is carrying my son Kos, who is still suckling, while my son Blia, who is still very small, is walking alone. We are separated from my other children, and I wonder with concern if they are still alive. For now, my concern, is to bring my four children who are with me to safety, walking carefully and slowly because my little ones have trouble keeping up.

There are bushes everywhere. You have to proceed step by step to avoid getting scratched: I stand in front, push the bushes aside, pass by, firmly holding the bush aside with the help of my daughter Zeu, and then light the way so that the little ones can pass. We move like that, bush after bush, obstacle after obstacle.

The rain begins to fall heavily. The mosquitoes circle around us and are already celebrating to be able to feed on the fresh blood of my children. At one point, I can no longer move forward. There is a huge bush blocking the way. I start to pray to my great grandparents and ask for their help. I promise them a meal in their honor and to burn some incense to thank them. Miraculously, I manage to push aside the huge bush that opens onto a rice field that its owners visibly abandoned. However, there is nothing to shelter us, so we continue walking in line and reach a small path. At the crossroads, I do not know which way to take since everything leads to this road. I decide to continue by chance, but my anxiety increases as we approach the main road, where the danger is much more present: the enemy could be waiting for us at the end of the path…

I tell myself: "We are certainly all going to die, mother and children…"

But I cannot give up for them and I keep going: "If we are to die tonight, we should die with dignity."

We walk along a plain where rumors are circulating that it is the home of a huge man-eating tiger. But my survival instinct is stronger than all these fears of the tiger, the Viet Cong, and the spirits, and we continue to the crossroads where, fortunately, no one is waiting for us. With a surge of courage, we cross another field of corn and sugar cane to finally reach the village of Haï Hong, where there is total excitement. Alerted by a young man who escaped from the shooting, the inhabitants enthusiastically prepare their departure. They thresh rice, kill chickens to stock up on provisions, and avoid leaving any meat for the enemy.

Everyone wears several layers of clothing to avoid carrying them on their backs. When they see us appear, they jump on us to question us:

"Should we be afraid tonight?"

Having barely recovered and relieved to find other living beings, I answer:

"I don't know. If they chased us, I have fear. But we didn't see them, and if they had chased us, they would have already been here. But I can't guarantee anything…"

Then, the village chief declares:

"Let's stay here tonight. Tomorrow, we will decide whether to leave."

Despite the hunger, the rice tastes like soaked semolina, and the meat has no taste. My eldest children and I settle at the village chief's house for the night. Our clothes are still wet, and we sleep without blankets. The night is restless because of the horrible cold despite the protection of the house. Outside, fleas bite the horses' legs, and the stamping of their hooves sounds like gunshots that prevent us from sleeping.

We spend the whole night in fear. It is only the next day at daylight that everyone realizes that the Viet Congs have not pursued us. After breakfast, the village men put the little ones on their backs and accompany us back to Phao-Khao. On the way, the news of the shooting has gone around the villages. "There are two wounded. Two boys." I shudder: "Are these my two guys?" "Indeed, a bullet went through my son Tseu's knee, but the other boy is my sister-in-law's son, and he is in the hospital. After hearing the story of the survivors of the shooting, Vang Pao's men set off to chase down the Viet Cong, who had long since fled.

4

In 1975, we learn that the war is over[7]. People began to flee everywhere. Those who had fought alongside the Americans had to hide or had to leave. Our village had become the path the fugitives passed through.

Soon, only four families are left in the village: the family of Blia Tchong, Txi Tchou, Grandfather Noa, and our family. And a dog that never stopped barking in the distance like a funeral eulogy.

Tou returned and put on his civilian clothes again, and we live by cultivating the fields, even if our hearts are no longer in it. The comings and goings of the inhabitants make the older ones envious. The younger ones are too young and unaware of the dramatic events that affect our daily lives. But Tou decides that we must stay, despite the warnings of friends and relatives: he cannot abandon my brother-in-law Tcha Yia, who is seriously ill. Weakened by his illness, he is unable to move. We try everything for days, but he still cannot eat to gain strength. Tou ends up invoking

---

7 In May 1975, American soldiers left Laos, marking the end of the Vietnam War. A period of repression against pro-Americans followed.

the spirits during a "*hu plig*[8]" ceremony. He asks forgiveness for an illness of which he does not know the source and promises an offering if the sick person regains a taste for food before daybreak. The spirits respond positively to his prayer.

During the night, I hear someone busy in the kitchen. It is my brother-in-law's wife:

"What are you doing so late?"

She answers me, pointing at her husband with her head: "He says he's hungry."

The next day, after several meals, my brother-in-law already stands on a cane.

Tou disappears when he senses danger and reappears when it moves away. It is the same for all men. Only women, children, and the elderly can move around freely and live as if nothing had happened. The repression has not yet reached here, and fugitives who have returned from their escape report that battles are raging in a village called Hin Heu.

For two months, my daughters and I continue cultivating the cornfields, as if everything is normal. The remaining inhabitants are Hmong who have accepted the doctrine of the Pathet-Lao: they are called the Red Hmong. Some people like us have no choice and are not yet worried by the new government.

One day, however, Tou's cousin, Aunt Gua-Ning, also a shaman, hears it say that "the man who wears the red headdress is the enemy of the people" and "wherever he goes, he'll soon be arrested and shot."

---

8 *Hu plig*: "Recalling the soul": a ceremony to soothe the soul. See Health care section.

There is no doubt that Tou is being referred to. He is the only one in the village who wears a red headdress when he practices his shamanic incantations.

Immediately after, Tou and my son Pheng leave for Na-Sou, asking us to wait for their instructions, which soon followed: we must leave too.

It is a huge shock. The separation is difficult to accept, and everybody wants to keep a souvenir of the other. It is while sharing the photographs that my eldest son Guia, angry, gives his wife a blow with his machete, which she still bears the scar on her forehead. Finally, all the photos are burned so the men can no longer be recognized.

To avoid being caught, we decide to share the children: the two eldest girls leave with their great aunt and the youngest leave by car. However, the barriers are reinforced on the roads and around the airports. People start to be arrested and put in prison. The hope of being able to leave in a good condition, slowly fades: it is now impossible to get through.

For a while we go back and forth between several villages, in the hope of being able to cultivate opium and to be able to afford clothes. But the Viet Cong dictate their laws, and seeing no way out, we return to Na Sou a short time later.

On the way back, we meet Vietnamese; some are on stretchers.

"You look like you have been stabbed," someone remarks.

"We were living peacefully, and the resistance fighters came down from the mountain and hammered us with their knives."

Some are frightening to see: their faces and legs are mutilated. We take turns overtaking each other...

My daughter Nadia, curious, follows them closely. When the ground is too unstable, they stop, and the wounded are carried by the unharmed to get through the difficult areas.

*

In Na-Sou, where we stay for a month, we discover huge abandoned fields, and all we have to do is harvest the rice to prepare good meals. Here, we eat plenty and can stay for a long time since there are enough vegetables and rice. However, the officials have set up two visa application campaigns to leave the country. After a month, they invite us to go to a village to apply for our visa: "Tomorrow morning, you will go to Pa-Ning at 7:00 am to apply for your visa."

We answer yes, but we know very well that it seems like a trap, and that night, we leave the village to join our cousins who live in Pu-Nieu, where we also stay for a month. Without money and with our clothes in shreds, we work for some permanent inhabitants of the village to be able to get a few bags of rice.

We still live in fear, and a sedentary life is dangerous for the whole family. The men make an absolute decision: we must leave everything and try to reach Thailand.

On November 22, 1975, we finally leave this

village.

It is around 11:00 pm that we head towards the forest. We remain hidden in the mountain all night long until the rooster crows. Then we slowly descend towards the valley; all day long, we walk in a column, one behind the other, and finally reach the valley around 5:00 pm. As night falls, we decide to take a break. Where we rest, we are surrounded by three hills and a small stream flowing down below. We put our luggage down where we can, out of breath from our walk. We do not look around to see if anyone is missing.

A nephew has just left to relieve himself; no one has seen him go away. Gnay-Vang and his family have just arrived and tell us:

"We saw someone a little further up who went to relieve himself; we don't know. Let's hope it wasn't the Viet Cong who followed us. We don't have to worry too much, we are going to sit down and prepare dinner."

The person had barely finished saying this when someone emerged from the bamboo.

Two girls who do not have children and who always stay away from us for fear that our children will draw their attention to them immediately start screaming:

"It's the Viet! They have a machine gun!"

Everyone runs away in one second. Exhausted by the journey, I ask Tou's opinion:

"Should we also run away?"

"No, we're not running away. We have children,

and we can't run away like this. We might die here."

My son Blia, who was cutting bamboo shoots to cook them, ran away as quickly as a hare, leaving only a flip-flop stuck in the mud of the stream.

The girls did not look carefully: when the nephew returned from doing his business, he pushed aside the bamboo blocking his path, which looked like a man holding a machine gun.

Exhaustion and fear make everyone nervous, and we imagine that we are surrounded by enemies ready to appear at any moment.

During the night and the following day, the adults try to gather everyone together. Unfortunately, my son Blia is missing. When everyone departs, it is with a heavy heart that we decide to continue our journey, unable to bring ourselves to stay and wait for him or to turn around to check if he has not returned to civilization[9]. We fear that the men will be captured and shot.

Since we left the village, I have been feverish and shivering throughout my body. Fear is stronger than pain in this humid forest, and I drag myself along, my back aching, ready to succumb. I suddenly become unable to walk, and my two sons, Guia and Pheng, carry me in turns. When one carries my luggage, the other carries me. But my son Guia is small, my feet drag miserably on the ground, and my body sways, which makes me vomit constantly. Despite my thinness, I am a burden to carry, and my sons

---

9 "*Returning to civilization*" means accepting to live under communist rule.

continually take turns to be able to hold on.

After a few hours of walking, I start to complain, saying to Tou: " *Kov txiv*[10], I am throwing up too much, it is better to leave me here. If I live, I will go and join the Viet Cong, if I die, too bad." And Tou replies:

"Ah, if we do that, we will all die! The boys will continue to carry you!"

My boys obey courageously, especially since everyone is in the same situation. We form a single file, like ants carrying their most precious possessions. With fear in their bellies, the strongest carry the weakest or the sick.

Gnay-Vang carries his mother, Gua-Ning carries her blind son, who is already a teenager, and my sons carry me...

Xang, Guia's son, starts to babble. When we arrive at exposed places, everyone is scared to death and whispers while trembling; he starts to talk, so everyone avoids them, afraid that we will be spotted.

"Go ahead or stay behind," they all say. After the village of Na-Nyos, they walk behind us, so far behind that we are surprised not to see them coming. Worried, I say to Tou: "We have already lost a boy; if we also lose our son and his family, what is the point of continuing?"

Tou and I decided to stop with our children and

---

10 The wife calls her husband *kov txiv*, literally "your husband", the husband calls his wife *kov niam* (pronounced *koa nia*), literally "your wife". These expressions are widely used by couples, as a sign of mutual respect.

wait for them. After a long time, we are relieved to see them finally arrive. However, after a few hours, the others ask them to walk ahead. Unable to do otherwise, they head towards the Mekong while we wait for them to get a little ahead to break camp.

To avoid being spotted, we walk at night, in the moonlight. My son Pheng, to help with his back, puts me on a blanket that he drags while I cling to his shoulders. Suddenly, he stumbles on a branch and lets go of me. I start to roll down the slope towards the ravine, and it is with a superhuman effort that he manages to get me out of there and put me back on his back. Sometimes, when he is almost out of strength, I put my head on his shoulder to become one with him and walk to lighten his load.

Finally, we arrive at the river. We distinguish two human shapes heading towards us, with a quick and sudden step, we drop our luggage and start running in all directions, thinking that they are Viet Cong. Fortunately, once again, it is only a false alarm. They are Guia, his wife, and their son. We are happy to find them alive. They say that they were hosted by Laotians and that they found a way to cross the river. We have to contact the Thais on the other side of the Mekong. But for days, attempts to contact them have been unsuccessful: no one can reach them.

We settled not far from the bank so we won't miss the signals from the other side. The Viet Cong continue to look for us: we follow the river and go down two hills, then settle in a place far enough away so they will not find us. Everyone is terrified, and there is nothing to eat. The boys go to pick papayas from the Laotians to feed those who are still able to eat. The weakest, like me, can no longer swallow anything. We can only lick some leftover chili peppers to get a taste of it and swallow a few grains of rice with a bit of water. That's all.

My fever will still not go down until the day Aunt Gua-Ning's children dig in the earth, looking for roots, discover some wild potatoes, and offer them to me. That night, everyone except me fell ill from drinking the soup made with this root. Instead, the illness suddenly leaves me. Relieved of the fever, I can finally sleep through the night.

For four days, we wander from place to place without finding a way to cross the Mekong. We only owe our survival to another fugitive and his family who, having arrived long before us, managed to build a bamboo raft and reach the other bank. During this time, my sons continued to steal food from the farmers in the area. Finally, one night, the Thais were warned of our presence and came to pick us up in January 1976. After distributing a bowl of rice to the children and the weakest, they drove us to Pa-Son and then Vinay. These are refugee camps where exiles like us are crammed into shacks made of straw.

Hmong from the Vang clan recruited Tou, who arrived well before us and worked for the Thais. He goes to work with them all day and barely earns 20 baht[11], but this allows us to buy a few vegetables and a few cigarettes for himself. We only have a little

---

11 Baht: Thai currency. 1 Bht = $0.297

rice with a tasteless broth for our only meal, and we don't eat enough. In the forest, we managed to capture a few animals, but in Thailand, you need money for everything. My sons set traps to catch field mices to get a little meat. Thanks to these little creatures, we regain our strength. However, we remain poor and live cloistered at home.

When people ask at parties: "Don't you have any young girls to go "*pov pob*[12]?"

I answer shamefully with a big smile to hide my shame: "We have some, but they don't like it."

People do not answer, but they know it is not true: all young people love the New Year's party to meet other young people their age.

How can I allow my daughters to go out when they have nothing to wear? I know it is not fair for them, but I must be firm.

Fortunately, our situation is improving through hard work, without being definitively better.

We live day after day without hoping for a better tomorrow.

One morning, my son Guia hears that a family, who has got his visas to France, does not want to go.

They say that France is an old country and people work very hard, in the forest. Why leaving for a country that is worse than Laos?

---

12 *Pov pob*, "ball toss", a game of seduction in which young men and women throw a small cloth ball at each other. More information in Section *New year*.

Tou decides to apply for. No matter the country, the purpose is to quit this place. His request is accepted and soon, we live the camp.

*

Here in Castres, we finally see the sun.

We can eat our fill and rest without having to work in the fields.

Tou does not want his children to be separated; that is why we left, leaving his brothers and sisters[13] in Thaïland.

We are alone, far from the other Hmong people. We are separated from other families and can not even invite each other to eat.

We live in solitude.

---

13 The brothers and sisters are from the Lis family, symbolizing the Hmong community and past life.

About the end

This is how my mother's story ends.

Not a word about her feelings and her difficulties integrating. Not a word about her loneliness, moments of doubt about our future, or deep feelings.

The most important thing, she concludes, is that we stay together and continue to love each other.

Maiv
Like a memory

Chronology

May 1975: End of the Vietnam War in Laos
Oct. 1975: Departure from Na-Sou village to Pu-Nieu
Nov. 1975: Departure from Pu-Nieu
Arrival at the Mekong after 8 days.
Camping on the river bank for 4 days
Jan. 1976: Pa-Son refugee camp
July 1976: Moving to Ban Vinay Camp
March 1977: Departure for France
Apr. 1977: Moving to Barre de Cévennes, then Florac
Summer 1977: Moving to Castres
1984: Moving to Draveil

Talking about May

1970. They say I was born on a rainy night behind the house. My father is absent, as he is most of the time. My mother gave birth to me, alone, with the help of a relative. At the same time, there was a death in the family. Was this a message? That my whole life would be a struggle?

I have been told. But I prefer to romanticize that part of my life. I prefer to say that I was born with my first memory. You know, the memory of an innocent, happy childhood.

Fate has its own way and shapes our lives to convince us to overcome adversity and make us who we are. The important thing is not the target, but the journey. However, nobody told me I had a choice. Had I known, I would have lived, instead of surviving: every day is like an endless lesson in life.

1

In the mountains, in the middle of the forest, a plain surrounded by hills. It has been dry for several days. The air is unbreathable, and the sun is relentless. We are playing by the river, totally carefree. Laughter by the stream.

We are running through the dusty soil when suddenly thunder rumbles, and large droplets start falling. The first drops hitting the land transform into clouds, suspending just a little above the ground before waterspouts pour furiously down on us. Without missing a beat of this miraculous rainfall, we grab our jars to cover the holes in the ground where the insects hide to protect from the heat; there are also some in the tree trunks. To avoid drowning, they come out and get trapped in the jars, and we just need to put the cap back on. It is how we manage to harvest some proteins, offered by nature.

Is this vivid memory really a memory at all? Or is it just my imagination?

When you have no memories, it is as if you never existed. I like to hold on to such events, which, despite their insignificance, are invaluable to me.

*

One morning, my mother asked me, "Are you coming with us to the fields?" I was surprised she suggested I go with her, along with my sisters and aunts. She keeps such a distance that I can only interact with her by nodding. There are no other relationships possible: she is always gone. Besides, I do not know about a mother's love, neither people hate. I am really innocent and save from fears.

So there we go, together, to discover new and distant lands, at least for me. It is a day's walk into the mountains. We walk along dirt paths made by the bare feet of farmer workers who have passed this way a thousands of times. I am not aware of their daily struggle to navigate these roads and tall grasses. I am just captivated by the verdant landscapes I am seeing for the first time in my life.

When we arrive at our destination, there is no need to tell me: hills of poppy fields with blood-red flowers on large stems and colorful leaves lie before my eyes.

Above it, like an enormous canopy, a blue sky with a few cumulus clouds. The hills, as far as the eye can see, are separated from the sky by poppy flowers that seem to hold it up proudly, with incredible strength. On the right side, a small house stands out in the middle of this extraordinary landscape.

"We are going to sleep there", says my mother, pointing to the little house on the hill.

I look at her with astonished eyes that say, "Really?"

I think it is the first time I have slept away from home. We set up the things we had brought from the village. Dinner is made and eaten right away. We quickly get into bed on improvised straw mattresses. When I look outside, the night is already dark. The sky, with its thousands of stars, gives me a strange feeling I never felt before. I suddenly understand that this moment is unique. I decide to keep it like a paint on my memory.

The following day, barely awake, my mother ordered me: "Go and get me the bowl outside, behind the window."

I obey, rubbing my eyes and head for the only window in the house. Everyone is already getting prepared to make the most of the day. I will remember my whole life when I discover the bowl in which icy cold water has frozen overnight. I never knew such a thing could happen. My mother, amazed at my discovery, explains that it is colder in these mountains at night. However, I felt nothing different the night before: my childhood sleep is stronger.

Throughout the day, I stay in the poppy fields with the workers, intoxicated by their fragrance, a bitter mixture of dew, and the freshness of these colorful mountains. The work involves making three cuts in the shell to release a bitter juice, which is left to dry before being collected with a small blade. This substance is called "opium," and the Hmong use it to treat many illnesses. I will later learn that many farmers abandon their rice or corn fields for the more profitable opium fields. The harvest is sold to the Laotian and the Chinese people, making them richer. So do my grandparents also, the job is easier and worth it.

And yet, my aunts will never see the color of opium money. My grandmother keeps the gold and silver ingots out of sight. Only once a year, my aunts get a new outfit for the New Year's celebration, and that is enough. They wear the same clothes throughout the year and don't even take them off to sleep. Kept away from knowledge, perhaps to make them more submissive, the girls are ignorant of style and the use of any beauty products, including soap.

They work from morning to night, along with my mother and older sisters, without ever complaining.

The children, for their part, are left to their own devices and live freely, without restraint. My early childhood is quiet and peaceful in the green mountain of the countryside. There are vast orchards of fragrant clementine blossoms and paths along the paddocks of my grandfather's horses.

We are free to go wherever we want, and the adults tell us stories of caves inhabited by monsters, of forests where child-devouring tigers prowl, of chasms where, since ancient times, dragons have lived quietly, waiting for a child to venture into their burrows and eat them alive... The rivers are populated by sea monsters that swallow children, so the adults only have their eyes left to cry. These stories keep us away from these dangerous places, and no one considers leaving the village.

To illustrate the danger that can be found anywhere, we are told the story of my aunt. One day, they are all out in the fields, and my aunt needs to relieve herself. To avoid being seen, she moves out of sight. She starts to settle down when suddenly the ground slips under her weight, and finds herself at the bottom of a lightless ravine. The ravine is covered in vegetation and creepers, so she did not see it. My uncle dreadfully managed to reach her and bring her to the surface on his back. Since then, my aunt has been a quadriplegic. It is a difficult time for my uncle and the whole family. When misfortune strikes one family member, everyone is affected, so much so that the balance holds in each member who makes up the household.

*

One day, my mother suddenly leaves the house. I am surprised by this sudden departure. Adults always want to protect children by keeping the truth from them, but not knowing is worse... She stays away for several days. When coming back, her face defeated, her eyes and cheeks hollowed out. I do not question her because children should not ask questions; a child should just be a child. They must live in ignorance from childhood, the most beautiful period of all.

Some time later, we hear a helicopter approaching. I have never seen one, but when I want to get a closer look at this machine that kicks up so much dust, they make me put my head down and tell me not to move. I see my mother coming out of the house, and despite the noise of the propellers furiously stirring the air and kicking up dust, I hear her cry of pain. A mother knows, even without a single word, that it is her son's body being brought back to her.

My brother Tseu died at the city's hospital, where my mother spent several days and sleepless nights praying to the spirits for his recovery. He is the third child in the family. He is one of the most handsome, and I will later learn that it is acute peritonitis that killed him. But my parents thinks it is a curse. Someone ill-intentioned had cast this "*tso pob zeb*[14]" spell on him, which would have been fatal.

It is the first death in my family. I do not understand much, not knowing what death means. I am forbidden to look at my brother's cold, lifeless body. People say that children's souls are sensitive and more easily "captured" by evil spirits. The latter are looking for the slightest misstep by the living to make them ill.

Children are kept away from the funeral ceremonies. They are told to remain quiet and not run or make noise. If they stumble, the evil spirits catch their souls, and adults are good at performing a "*hu plig*" ceremony to bring them back into their bodies. I have heard of a child who tripped at a funeral and was ill for a very long time... So, I listen quietly to my brothers.

---

14 *Tso pob zeb* : "Throw a pebble", sow evil in small doses. It's a spell that some people cast for revenge, out of jealousy or spite.

My grandfather, devastated by grief, gives him two slaps that took everyone by surprise, in the hope, with no doubt, that he will wake up. But death took him from his family.

A few days later, my older sisters, as they roamed the fields, remembered with nostalgia his joy of life, his laughter, and his songs, which made everyday life less difficult for everyone.

2

My great-grandfather came from China, along with his brothers. His name was Blia Txia. Driven into exile by territorial conflicts with the settled populations of their mountains, many Hmong families left their lands to settle in Southeast Asia. My 19th-century ancestors settled in the mountains of Laos, cultivating the highlands where they made a reputation that continues to serve their descendants nowadays.

In our village, my grandfather Say Txong is a well-known and relatively wealthy landowner. He is the patriarch of a beautiful family. It is common practice to have as many children as nature can give. My grandfather had two wives: after the death of the first, he married a second and, in total, had four sons and four daughters. A main clan generally inhabits each village, as a family provides mutual aid that is part of everyday life. The family owns animals: pigs, chickens, dogs, and horses. Nothing goes to waste, and I remember one day, one of the horses died and ended up as a meal.

For me, it was impossible to eat. At that time, we do not suffer from hunger yet, even though we are in a time of war, we live peacefully in our countryside and are not suffering the consequences of the events shaking Southeast Asia. There is talk of conflicts involving certain Hmong personalities and then of civil war, but the Hmong living in the mountain continue to fight against their ancestral enemy: hunger. It is a struggle for survival, and most people are not interested in politics or what is happening around them.

Yet history eventually caught them in its whirlwind. Soon after the Indochina War, which ended French colonization, the Vietnam War followed. The U.S. Army set up its secret base in Laos to deploy its planes over Vietnam.

My father and my older brothers work for the American Army. All the men are enlisted to serve this country called *Amelika*[15]. Without knowing where this country is, there is a particular pride in being a soldier and serving a cause for which the leaders say it is good to serve. A few photos are taken of the peasants in military costumes, with berets and rifles, and with smiles on their faces. At first, it is a bit of the euphoria of the American dream that wins the countryside and promises the poor that they will have their place in a better world. Then things start to change, little by little. People die, and others disappear. The word "war" is whispered. The women are afraid when the men leave.

For years, the fighting intensifies. Families are

---

15 Hmong does not pronounce the letter "r", so it is replaced by the "l".

divided: there are the "reds[16]" who want to liberate the country from the invading enemy, and there are the "traitors[17]" who have joined the enemy. Whichever side they are on, there is a kind of incomprehension for those who want to live in peace. As in all conflicts, propaganda brings fear and death.

The guerrilla war rages on. The men have all left. Women and children are trying to survive in a chaotic country and are among the collateral victims. My Aunt Ma lost her young son, killed before her eyes by the Viet Cong during a surprise raid. My uncle, who had joined the group of fighters battling the invading enemy, discovered him abandoned in the house, sprawled out on a straw mat, covered with a sheet.

He digs his child's grave himself and buries him in this abominable hole, which he covers with earth, in the most unbearable suffering. For years, he refuses to leave the country so as not to leave his son alone in the middle of plains that will soon be spread with bombs. Why, he has often asked himself?

"We were told we had to take up arms to defend our country until the Chiefs returned," but the Chiefs left for America a long time ago, and he does not know it yet, but they will never come back to save little soldiers like himself.

After several years of waiting, my uncle finally gives up his weapons and joins the fugitives on their way to Thailand.

---

16 The "reds" means communists.
17 The "traitors" are the Hmong who work for the USA Army.

*

The Viet Cong threaten to capture all pro-Western fighters. Entire families pack their belongings and leave in buses chartered by the American government, transporting their compatriots and allies. It is May 1975. America has capitulated and is bringing its troops home, leaving their Hmong allies to their fate. Those who follow are the bureaucrats and the wisest.

At first, my father decides to stay in the village with the whole family. Neither my grandfather nor my uncle thought of leaving either. My uncle Dchoua Nou says: "Even if there are only ants left, I'll stay here with them."

Faced with everyone's hesitation, my parents decide to stay, especially as my uncle Blia Xiong cannot leave with his quadriplegic wife.

My sisters continue to work in the fields, watching with envy those who leave for a better life: lines of families and entire clans pass through the village.

Tension and fear of repression begin to spread throughout the countryside. The villages are empty, the fields deserted. Realizing that danger is closing in on us, my father decides we must flee, too. His decision sounds like a death sentence. My heart is pounding. Suddenly, my little world collapses, and I am afraid for the first time in my life. The adults seem so serious suddenly: their voices break, their gestures are quick, and they stress as they gather clothes and knick-knacks into makeshift bags.

From that moment on, we become fugitives, hiding

from village to village. To buy food, my parents take on occasional jobs: in a paper factory, where they dry tobacco outside before collecting it, then assemble and cut it for packaging. We ended up joining my father's family in Pu-Nieu in October 1975. Then, during a ceremony, my aunt hears that my father is being targeted for an ambush. This time, we leave for good.

During the night, we are awakened. We head into the forest for what will prove to be an interminable march.

I discover the hunger, the cold, and the fear that will never leave me. I am startled by every sound, but I courageously follow the line of men, women, and children on this path that goes deeper and deeper into the forest. The leaves' thickness and the plants' density mask the daylight. Only a few rays, miraculously breaking through, let us know it is daytime. My eyes are fixed on the back of the person I am following, while those of the adults are on the lookout for the slightest glimmer of light; it is in this grey world that we move forward.

At a bend in the path, the sun breaks through the thick leaves to draw a comforting halo of light on the ground, like the hope of seeing the end of this forest. My mother, who has been dragging her sick body around with her since we left, settles into the beam for a moment to take in some warmth. Footprints resembling those of a tiger suggest that the latter has passed this way and could return, but never mind! We are not afraid of this wild animal, but of our fellow human beings on our heels. Children, the elderly, the sick, and the disabled, all of us are on the run with fear in our bellies. It is in despair that man rediscovers the primary survival instinct. I think that is what guides adults.

Despite our differences, there is a kind of solidarity that compels us to stay together and walk in silence. Even the delirium caused by the fever has been silenced, to the detriment of agonizing suffering that adds to the pain of aching bodies, battered for days on end.

The night also brings its own doubts. When we stop to sleep in the evening, my dreams take me back to our long walk, like a nightmare movie where someone with malicious intent is playing repeatedly, with no end in sight. How can you close your eyes when the enemy can appear anytime?

Men carry within them the weight of our survival. Always on the alert, they take turns in front and behind us to cover our march.

One day, we come upon an orange river torrent. The waters surge mercilessly over the rocks, and in places, their reddish foam stains the shore a blood-red hue. To cross, a fragile-looking monkey bridge is stretched across. Planks no wider than a child's small foot are clumsily hung to secure each span. After consultation, there is no other solution but to cross the bridge. Given the state of fatigue of the weakest, it is inconceivable to turn back or to follow the river to find another way out. Nature reigns supreme, and the banks are inaccessible, overgrown with vegetation as dense as wild. One by one, we make our way across the shaky bridge with unsteady steps. When it is my turn, fear grips me. With my hands on the ropes, my foot struggles to reach the other plank: it is hard to balance because the bridge keeps pitching and the plank seems out of reach. But I have got to get across, so I take a deep breath of air before plunging bravely forward and, with difficulty, manage to make headway. Between the planks, the tumultuous flow seems to draw closer, the better to swallow me. The bridge wobbles, and I tremble with all my limbs before realizing that others are following me with the same uncertainty.

Suddenly, in front of me, a girl starts screaming. Her foot is caught between two planks. We are yelled at to stop moving. The moment of panic lasts only a few seconds before a man on the bridge retraces his steps to help the unfortunate girl, placing his foot parallel to the planks. Meanwhile, the moment is an eternity for those already engaged on the bridge; the uproar of the waves resembles a battle, and the noise they make, the cries of thousands of angry pursuers...

Finally, one by one, we land on the other bank, safe, but there is no break for the fugitives. Above all, we must not remain in the open and continue on our way. But where to? The younger ones are obliged to remain silent, and we follow the exhausting march that never ends, haggard and hungry. Besides, I have never been curious enough to know why we are running away. Our parents have told us to leave, so we obey without question, aware of the gravity of the situation.

When we see the hard stares of our fathers, who impose absolute silence on us for days and nights on end, and our mothers making us meals of roots and leaves, we can only respect total obedience.

From time to time, a few words of encouragement are heard:

"We will be there soon."

No matter who says it, we believe it and intensify our efforts. Sometimes, we trample on our own footsteps and think they are those of our pursuers, but we end up recognizing our footprints: we have gone around in circles.

We often get lost and turn around with no horizon to guide us, but we continue to form a column, certainly on borrowed time but homogeneous.

I am carrying my father's gong, which almost completely covers my back; it is the gong he uses for his shaman ceremonies, and it is essential that I do not abandon it. As I am so small and frail, this is the only thing they could give me to carry. There are no useless backs. Everyone has to be able to help in their own way, to the best of their ability.

At night, we sleep restlessly, praying to some ancestor to wake us from this nightmare, which continues long after awoken.

When we come to a halt, the frontrunners are well rested and ready to set off again, while the back runners are not yet visible behind us...

*

After an interminable day of walking, we decide to take a break in the middle of a clearing. I sit next to my mother and watch my fellow travelers settle in: even the healthiest and most able-bodied look like wrecks. One after the other, they put down their luggage and throw themselves on the ground for a life-saving rest when suddenly someone starts shouting:

"Save yourselves! It's the Viet Cong!"

My heart leaps in my chest, and without trying to understand, I flee and run as fast and far as possible. Panicked cries echo through the clearing. Everyone is running in every direction, and the next thing I know, all that is left are the sick and the abandoned luggage. I find myself crossing a small stream in which my flip-flop gets stuck. Instinctively, I turn to retrieve it, but the person with me dissuades me.

"Leave it alone! You haven't got time! Run!".

I am being pulled by the arm. I think it is my brother Zo. We run, trying to stay together, as far away as possible, and when we feel we have gone far enough, we hide behind a small bush. The echoes of the runners resonate through the clearing.

We hardly dare to breathe and cling to the bush for hours, trembling with all our limbs. The forest is now morbidly silent. For a very long time, it seems like an eternity, we remain like this, huddled against the small bush, feeling neither hunger nor cold, but only this fear that will never leave us.

Around us, others also hid behind other bushes, but

like us, none of them moved. We hear our frightened hearts beating like drums; beating too loudly, inviting even the enemy to find us. Where are the others? My mother? My father? Are they all dead?...

My eyes anxiously examine the place where we came for fear of seeing the enemy appear. It must be our turn soon, they are definitely going to find us.

Then, voices begin to call in the distance, slowly approaching. We become even smaller, holding our breath as the words are confusing.

"Come back! It's a false alarm!" But we do not move, convinced it is a trap. They have caught the adults and are forcing them to lie to us. They want us to believe that everything is fine, but we do not believe them.

"It's not the Viet Cong," the voices insist! "You can come out!"

We are still suspicious and stick to our little tree that hides and protects us. Then, I see a familiar face come forward, and in the distance, other fugitives begin to emerge from their hiding places, recognizing their parents, brothers, and sisters.

Still trembling and unconvinced, my brother and I rejoin our people. Trust is hard to re-establish; the whole day consists of bringing everyone together, with difficulty. Late into the night, the men continue to search for my brother Blia, who must have run faster than any of us. The women have worn out their voices, but he is nowhere to be found, and my mortified parents are condemned to carry on without him...

Now with heavy hearts and no hope of getting out of this forest, we reform our column and continue on our way, like little ants condemned to suffer bad luck.

Nerves are frayed and every unusual noise is suspect. We have not been quiet since the start of this leak, and we are even less so now. My parents walk but their mind turn back, hoping to see my brother.

But hours later, they know that there is no chance to seeing him alive.

We must continue our walk, again and again...

Suddenly, another cry startles us and a voice invites us to run away again. But the older ones are resigned and refuse to move. Fortunately, it is my brother Guia and his family who come back to warn us that they have found a road leading to the Mekong.

That is where the adults want to take us: they say we will be free on the other side.

Once again, families form small groups and continue on their way, while men sometimes disappear for several hours. They always return with rice, chickens, eggs, or fruit.

I later learn that they steal from the farmers, otherwise, how else?

Finally, after several hours, we arrive in front of an immense river with frightening swirls. Perhaps less than the one we crossed a few days earlier. It seems less threatening without the red color and the monkey bridge, but it is just as dangerous. It is the Mekong, the border river between Laos and Thailand.

But we must continue to live hidden in the bushes or under the trees, slightly back, to avoid the dangerous glances of our enemies who, it seems to us, continue to search for us. After four days, we begin to suffer from hunger. My brothers and a few men set off inland to collect food. Then, the smugglers finally arrived. My parents are penniless and afraid to leave my brothers behind. They get into debt with my aunts to pay the price of our freedom.

The night of the crossing is dark. Everything is a shadow: the river, the trees, the roaring waves, the boats. The men are silhouettes like in a deaf and muted black-and-white film. Life-size shadow puppets projected under the rays of a pale moon. In any case, without it, the show would not happen. We all fear the worst, a drama that would end the march of the fugitives here. We settle into a makeshift boat: no one knows how to swim, and if it capsizes, the end is inevitable. We are not water people, we are mountain people. We have come a long way and pray that it is not to drown.

Fortunately, the river is merciful tonight. Even upstream, it lets the moon shimmer on its wrinkled surface, illuminating the ferrymen and their frightened passengers. The boats glide slowly over the waves, pitching gently as some choke the fear in their throats to keep it from coming out and frightening the others...

We land on the other side of the river, where we are signaled to cross the road and hide in the ravine, awaiting orders.

The smugglers turn their boats around to fetch the others. Our greatest fear is to lose one of us.

Finally, everyone is gathered, and morning is

already on the horizon. Together, we rise, haggard, and set out on the clay road that will lead us to our new home. The river remains unchanged, continuing its never-ending flow. The Laotian shore gently recedes from our view, carrying with it our dreams for the future, our hopes for a better life, the history of our ancestors, our deaths, and, above all, our escape. But not our fear.

Here, on this clay soil, we all tread for the first time, and our life of exile begins.

*

Rows of tents stuck together in the refugee camp, called Pa-Son. Social differences are reflected in the wealth each person has brought back from Laos. The well-off families are those with smaller siblings and those who have been here for a long time. They benefit from the camp's experience: the resourcefulness and opportunities save the bravest.

Our parents do not have the right to rest. They have to start looking for food again. They leave nothing at odds in this new environment. Taking their courage in both hands, they disdains no thankless task. You have to work for the other Hmong for a few grains of rice? They turn the soil, weed, plant, and harvest without complaining. We will forget it too quickly later, but our parents give us everything during those months in the camp.

Then, we are drived to Ban Vinay[18], another refugee camp, where we remain for a year.

They continue work like slaves for other more fortunate refugees who have managed to obtain a garden for a small sum of money, but that does not stop us from going hungry.

There is a big lake near the camp, and my father often goes fishing with the other men. The water comes up to their waists. Some of them hold on to the net, which they stretch out in a circle, while others, facing them, pull in the trapped fish, which try to save themselves by throwing their bodies uselessly outwards. However, these efforts only weaken them, and they lie on top of each other in the net, much to the children's amazement.

We eat them every day until a fishbone gets stuck in my throat. I vomit up to the bile. For a long time, with each swallow, I can still feel it piercing my throat.

On rainy days, the aisles are full of mud; on dry days, dust is part of what we breethe. There is no possibility of a better world; we really live day by day. Tomorrow will undoubtedly be similar to today.

In this overcrowded village, life is organized to look like something normal. Tonight, a film I do not know the title, is shown on a huge screen set up in the square. It is the first time I have been to this kind of event. There is a lot of excitement. The crowd gathers around the oversized screen. Everyone's head is turned towards the screen, symbolizing a distant

---

18 Ban Vinay: at the height of its occupation, this camp housed over 45,000 refugees, most of them Hmong.

and inaccessible West.

Here, there are no fields to cultivate. The children continue to live with the carefree spirit of their age, and we sometimes wander around the camp or go swimming at the lake. I am a pretty good swimmer, and my friend and I often go swimming. I trap the air with my Laotian skirt and use it as a buoy. When I realize that my friend is far behind me, I get scared. I suddenly think of the dragons that live in the depths, and I am afraid they will drag my feet and take me away to live with them. That is the legend my mother tells me, probably so I do not move away from the shore. At that moment, her story has its effect, so I use my hands as flippers and quickly find myself on the other side of the lake.

My sisters do not go out much: they are young girls to be married off. There is no shortage of suitors. Bands of marriageable boys and girls parade through the huge, dusty square.

The boys in the family are sent to school. My sisters are not allowed to: they are reserved for housework and helping their parents. Being still young, my parents decide to try and send me to school.

Dressed in the costume of a Thai schoolgirl (a blue pleated skirt and white blouse), I show up at school one morning accompanied by a classmate. The teacher gives us an angry look, accompanied by a reprimand that still makes me shiver:

"Do you bring me something? You know you have to bring something if you want to come to school, don't you?"

We are very surprised: this is our first day at school and we do not s know this rule.

"Go away! Go and bring me some wood! If not, don't come back!"

We run away quickly, and while we search for logs neither too heavy nor too light, which can be used as heating, my thoughts race through my head.

I do not really want to go to school, and neither pay for that. After consultation with my friend, we decide never to set foot in school again. The teacher will not see the color of our wood. Our parents do not reprimand us; they have other things to worry about.

The days and months pass without the hope of a different tomorrow. Little by little, the camp empties for the benefit of new arrivals. Busloads transport fortunate families to the West, we are told: to the USA, France, and Canada... People leave each other crying. They all know that the likelihood of seeing each other again is slim. Yet, leaving the camp remains a privilege[19]. My father has applied for visas, but we do not have anyone abroad, and there is no indication that we will ever be able to leave this place.

On the day of the "calls", people gather around the authorities and stamp their feet with impatience and worry, divided between the joy of being called and the sadness of leaving their loved ones.

On the day of departure, dozens of buses are parked on the dusty red square, waiting for the lucky

---

19 The criteria for obtaining a visa are: having a relative in the host country or having served under the flag of the host country (see Jean-Pierre Willem's book "Les naufragés de la liberté").

ones who can leave the camp for a better life.

While attending the departure, those who stay feel a particular desire but are content to tell themselves that there is space available in the accommodation and that they can apply for it to improve their daily life until the next call. Luckily, my brother Guia report to my father that a family that has obtained a visa for France refuses to go there. They prefer America. It is the wish of many families.

For my father, the destination does not matter. All he wants is to get away from this dusty life. Even though rumors say that France[20] is a backward country, even though people work in the fields, as they do in Laos, as hard as they used to when we lived in peace, he decides to try his luck by signing us up as volunteers to go to France.

---

20 Many Hmong were repatriated to French Guiana and, by dint of their own strength, managed to make the forests cultivable. Today, the community is a major player in Guyana's economy.

3

March 1977. My mother is forty-two, and my father is forty-eight. Finally, after a year of survival, we leave the Ban Vinay camp, which has become a village where precariousness and hygiene are becoming difficult to live in. My parents quickly packed a few items of sentimental value and pushed me onto the coach. We stay together: they are too afraid to leave one of us on the sidewalk. They quickly embrace the aunts, but there are so many relatives that the goodbyes take forever. The youngsters shed warm tears for their lovers, watching the camp move away, having become too small for the impressive number of refugees who arrive daily.

How long do we ride? I do not know, but I find myself on a plane. It is my first time in a "bird of steel."

When it rises, I cast fearful glances around me and realizing that I am not the only one to feel fear knotting my stomach, I snuggle into the back of my seat and let myself be guided by a round-eyed hostess. I am sick the whole way. My brain is stuck to my skull as if it wants to come out; my stomach empties of gastric juice down to bile.

They ended up giving me a medicine which, as soon as I swallowed it with difficulty (I have never swallowed medicine in my life), ended up taking effect. Barely asleep, I am carried to a seat in the front row.

The plane lands at Paris-Charles-de-Gaulle. We are located in a vacation center in Dourdan[21]. I do not remember how, but I find myself in a large room. We are seated around a table, and dozens of pairs of round eyes stare at us, whispering in a strange language. "*Fab kis*[22]" ladies are serving us a meal.

We are like little ants pouncing on a lump of sugar: as soon as the bread basket is placed on the table, it is already empty. The little savages that we are have grabbed several loaves per person, the slower ones only just recovering a loaf that they jealously guard in their dirty hands with bony fingers... The intestines, deprived of food for so many years, feel, with each piece swallowed, like a tear grazing their walls to land in the stomach, which seems to cry out with joy and never wants to be satisfied before being completely bloated.

This new environment frightens everyone. My first night in the camp is tinged with nightmares. As we are a large family, we were dispatched in two houses. During the night, unable to sleep, some of us get up and wander around like ghosts trying to chase us out of this house that is not ours...

This place, however, is only transitory. Settling

---

21 Little town situated near Paris, Essonne area.
22 Fab kis. Prononciation: fa ki, means French.

must be done in several stages. Shortly afterward, each family is sent to different locations. Ours is sent south to Barre-des-Cévennes. In this village deep in the French countryside, we live in a small house[23] where part of the entrance opens onto a balcony. From there, you can see the whole village below. Our new life is a new birth, during which our parents also relearn everything: cooking, drinking from a glass of water, going to the toilet...

But unlike us, they have to pretend to know, while we have the excuse of our youth; our ignorance can be forgiven, and learning is easier for us. The social workers have been looking after our integration since we arrived[24]. They are trying to find work for men and women who can work, but it is only temporary, as we know. We told them we came from the mountains and that most of us were farmers. But here, there is no land to cultivate. The adults are busy weaving wicker baskets and chairs: they are talented and learn quickly. The children do not go to school yet and play freely.

Members of the same family stay together: in my family, there are my parents, my brothers Pheng, Kou, Zo, and Yen, and my sisters Zeu and Nadia. Then, my brother Guia, his wife, and their son.

Sometimes, I accompany my mother to the washhouse a little further down. We scrub the laundry with soap, beat it with a big spatula, and wring it out

---

[23] The former gendarmerie has been converted into a home for refugees.
[24] See the book "*Ne me lâche pas la main*", by Cathou Quivy, a social worker who kept in charge the refugees.

by twisting it. It is hard on my little hands, but my mother lets me do it, probably just for the educational side. Then we carry the laundry in big basins to the terrace, where my mother dries it on ropes. It is on this terrace that the first photo is taken, with my parents, my sister Zeu, my brother Yen and me. Yen and I are seen with red hair due to a protein deficiency[25].

We do not wash much, and I hate it, especially as the shower is in the basement of the house: it is dark there. As soon as we get in, old, discarded fabrics and plastics start to float around like scaring shadows. I am a bit of a coward and I have far too much imagination: I immediately think of ghosts. When it is time to shower, the older rush in first and run back upstairs, leaving me alone in this darkness room where the slightest noise startles me. I often barely wet my hair and body, then quickly climb back among the living.

Other Hmong, who arrived earlier and speak French, serve as our guides. They handle our identity papers (political refugee cards and residence permits). Our dates of birth are approximate, and the spelling of our first names is not very accurate. But we will have to be content with these inaccuracies forever.

It is almost summer, and when there is nothing to do, we go for a walk in the hills to discover the area. The tall grasses are dry, the air is soft, and the heat has been present for several days. Nothing like the high Hmong mountains, where the forest stretches as

---

[25] Kwashiorkor disease: due to malnutrition, hair turn red, turn white and then fall out.

far as the eye can see. We can see the village and its surroundings from the top of the hills. In 1977, we listen to Laurent Voulzy[26] on the radio, which the men carry along on the walk. It is quite strange to hear "Rock Collection" echoing in the mountains...

One day, returning from our walk, we understand that something serious has happened. I feel my mother's heavy concern as she tells us that my brother Zo is in hospital. He has an open fracture in his arm. We are shown where the accident took place. He was sliding and caught his arm in the boards at the bottom of the slide. There are still a few fresh drops of blood.

"The bone came out," we are told.

It is awful to imagine. Zo pulls through but suffers unbearable pain afterward and is even excused from military service.

Some time later, we are drived to Florac, where we live in real houses in a vacation center that is still uncrowded due to the low season, it is April. A lady explains how to use the toilet: you have to climb onto the bowl, squat down, and do your business in the hole... It is hard to get your aim right while keeping your balance... In reality, this is, of course, not how we should proceed. Back home, there are no toilets, thus designated by "fab kis": we do it in nature. Besides, it is a detail that I do not remember anymore. Where was I going to relieve myself?

My older sister Zeu, aged seventeen, is sent to a campsite to clean to help the couple who owned the

---

26 Laurent Voulzy : famous French singer. His tube "Rockcollection" (1977) is still popular nowadays.

place. She cleans the toilets and takes care of the dirty work. Alone and isolated from the rest of us, she finds this situation very difficult, especially since she does not understand a single word from the two French people who, to give her instructions, point to the toilets or the showers. The instructions, which sound like orders, are like grunts, letting her know that this will be her task for the day.

She feels stupid, and the lack of consideration makes her so unhappy that she spends her nights crying.

My sister Nadia, who is a year younger than her, stays with us. She feels a deep loneliness. In Thailand, young girls were surrounded by young men who courted them, and Nadia was very courted. Today, she feels very lonely. She often takes refuge in the mountains to sing to them of her melancholy and solitude. A few months later, she accepts a marriage proposal from a man from the Vu clan whom she does not know. She thinks this will free her from the unappreciated household chores imposed on her by her parents: cleaning, washing, and cooking from morning until night. But arranged marriages are common, and no one is surprised. During this occasion, my sister Zeu returns temporarily to celebrate the wedding. Then, with a heavy heart, she returns to the couple's home, while my sister Nadia leaves with her husband, with whom she will live in the Paris region.

Then, we are sent to Castres, in the Tarn region, in the south of France.

The journey riding the coach is a nightmare for me: I vomit the whole way. They disembarked our family in the middle of the afternoon in a square full of curious people watching us like circus animals. It is in this city, they say, that we will begin our new life.

We are placed in the Bisséous tower[27], a fourteen story building planted in the middle of other blocks of buildings, surrounded by houses. We have never seen a tower so high in our lives: just by looking up, we feel dizzy as if the tower is crushing us with all its weight.

It is like a U-shaped in 3D, with living quarters in each wing. We are installed in the left wing, on the 9th floor, where we are taken up by a huge elevator that can carry a dozen people. The first time I get on it, I feel like all my internal organs are going up, and I stick to the wall. The nightmarish elevator never seems to want to stop.

The apartment has four bedrooms: one for my parents and Yen, one for Kou and Zo, one for the girls (I sleep with my sister Zeu), and one for Pheng (the living room is separated by a partition to make an extra bedroom).

The living room opens onto a balcony where we can see the roofs of the houses and gaze into the distance, where we can see the top of the trees. My sister and I sleep in the bedroom that faces inwards: the window is covered by blinds, and during windy periods, which is often the case (Castres is located

---

27 The Bisséous tower, deemed too dangerous, was demolished on August 29, 1999.

near the Mediterranean region), it is impossible to sleep. In this room, my sister and I live in a universe separated by age: at seventeen, deprived of her friends and peers, she spends her time nostalgically listening to songs of love and separation.

> "Winter is already here, where are you?
> *Ntuj no tuaj lawm kov nyob qhov twg*
> I can't sleep, I think of you
> *Kuv pw tsis tau tseem nco*
> I think of our love story...
> *Tseem nco txog wb txoj kev sib hlub* "

We live alone among other populations of color. Our minority is isolated in the tower district.

The other Hmong live in a district called "The littel train" on the other side of downtown. A few of them live on a farm a few minutes from us, while my brother Guia and his family live in a block of flats next to the playground.

My father has imposed rules of discretion: we must not make any noise, we must be discreet, so as not to cause any trouble. You have to blend in. It is already an immense opportunity to be here, alive and, above all, all together. It is difficult, for my parents as much as for us. Over there, we lived in freedom; we went wherever we wanted, without any curious eyes on us. In this apartment, the walls seem so thin that you almost have to whisper to avoid disturbing the neighbors I am afraid to bump into every time I go out. The contact and gaze of others become my greatest difficulty.

Before going out, I look through the peephole to see if there is any light in the corridor. If there is, I do not come out until it goes out. I am also terrified of the elevator because entering it is a ritual. To be polite, I have to ask the people entering at the same time as me, "Which floor?" I press the floor indicated by my "elevator companions", then wait. When I get out, I have to say "goodbye"... It is a real dilemma, and I often take the stairs. When I get to the first floor, to avoid running into anyone, I go through the garbage room, where the light switch is damaged, which causes me to have a few strokes of juice. But I would rather do that than meet the building superintendent's gaze.

The neighbor tries a few approaches, but you gasp and stop breathing when she knocks on the door. She is a nice lady with white hair and a lovely smile. She and her daughter manage to take us into her home to give us some clothes. Embarrassed and confused to receive so much attention, my parents were overwhelmed with endless thanks and bows.

We never go anywhere alone. To play at the foot of the tower, my two brothers, Zo and Yen, are always present. Like a boy, I frolic, climb trees, and climb my bike up a steep, narrow slope. A real daredevil! In summer, we watch TV and play cards with sweets and board games.

My father is learning French, while my mother, a faithful housewife, spends her time between cooking and embroidery. It is a complete change of life for the elders. From a distance, I can imagine how difficult it is for them to integrate, while the younger ones, who are still lucky, can learn with the little "*fab kis*".

Our guide, Mrs. Joffre, visits us quite often when we first settle in. It is like a holiday when she takes us to pick up clothes from a kind of social shelter or generous donors. We choose what we want and are eternally grateful to the people who give us such lovely cardigans, sweaters, blouses, coats, and many other useful things. At first, we do not know what this means because we do not yet know how to put our nudity, our daily hunger, and our lack of everything into words. When we finally discover the expression "to be poor", we also realize our material poverty. It is an unspeakable shame for us. And yet, knowing we are poor, watching others buy what they want, with envy, makes us feel different, and it is even worse.

We continue to survive on welfare for a long time. No unnecessary purchases are allowed. Everything is bought in large quantities and stored in the freezer. Few vegetables, lots of meat, especially pork, which is the cheapest, and chicken. Because we have missed so much, every meal is made up of large quantities of meat - if not, we are not satisfied... The chore of cutting the potatoes into fries is endless: we do not know frozen fries.

When we first moved in, the social workers took the adults shopping and helped them with all kinds of formalities (papers, letters, medical visits, finding a job...).

Teenagers and young adults are placed in

apprenticeships, while the youngest are enrolled in school.

So, my sister Zeu was sent on an apprenticeship and returned every weekend. But it was challenging for her, and after two months, she refused to go back to boarding school. So she learns sewing and, thanks to Mathilde, a social worker who helps us, gets hired by a not-very-honest boss who exploits her by doing her work on November 11th when there is no one else in the company.

My brother Kou goes to training to learn mechanics, my brother Zo goes to a school to learn French, my brother Yen goes to kindergarten, and I go to first grade.

4

From this moment I am left to be independent. I must become a whole person. Now, I have to think and to decide on my own. Living without the others members of my family makes me weak, because we are used to be strong all together.

The watchword rehashed by my father is "integration", whatever the cost. The brain must focus all its attention on learning the French language including habits and customs.

In this new fight where everyone is now alone, fear remains present and grows every day, even if it is not the same fear as during the flight. Living my own life, avoiding mistakes is frightening: what is an error, and what is not? How acting freely when I never learn to?

During this second birth, I attended the Bisséous school at 4 rue des Frères Nicouleau, opposite the rugby stadium. It is a co-educational school since boys and girls were allowed to study together; it is still written above the entrance doors "Boys" and "Girls": I am in the "Boys" school.

I remember my first day at school: I entered the classroom under pairs of curious eyes. The teacher, Mister Julien, a tall, lean, stern-looking man, motions for me to sit at a desk in the back row. I do not understand a word he is saying. My classmates look at me in whispers. They have never seen an Asian in their lives and are probably wondering where I am from and why I have wrinkled eyes. I feel uncomfortable because I feel like they are laughing at me.

In addition, it is first grade, which is a difficult time for little ones coming from kindergarten. It is an important year: learning to write, read, and math.

The morning is torture. I want to disappear and pray that it is all a dream, but the whispers and stares of the other children make me realize that what I am experiencing is real.

I remember bending over my writing notebook, holding my fountain pen ink black, and forming my first letter. The blackboard makes the "A" dance in all its forms between lines perfectly drawn by Mister Julien. His sharp eye watches for the slightest grimace that could appear on the little, youthful faces of his dear students, maybe for punishment in case they do not succeed. He is severe.

I skilfully copied this solitary work, but like a frightened animal that arouses the curiosity of others, I lurk in the corners of the yard during recess. At 11:30, someone asks me a question: "Do you eat at the cafeteria?" Not understanding anything, I smile stupidly, and the others take it for a "Yes." I am lined up and pressed up against a few laughing, whispering classmates, here I am, taken to the dining area, where I do not have time to sit down before an adult starts to pull me by the arm.

Jostled and feeling rejected, I find myself at the school entrance where my mother is waiting for me. She looks at me with angry eyes. She does not understand what has happened to me either. We walk slowly side by side, in silence.

From deep inside, I expect some comfort from her. I want her to explain things to me. We zigzag between streets and rows of buildings, before arriving at the tower, which I see approaching with relief.

I think my ordeal is over, but after lunch, she leads me again to school and leaves me to my fate. The ritual is repeated every day.

My father disappears from my daily life, as do my brothers and my sister. My mother would like to do the same and makes me feel it. I think everyone tries to hold on, not to weaken to show the other that we can get through it. But at what cost? My mother soon abandons me, judging that I am old enough to make the journey alone.

Thanks to attentive listening and my young age, I quickly learn the language. But I feel terribly alone and I make myself very small. I am afraid of everything, and as soon as someone speaks to me, I wish the earth would open up beneath my feet and make me disappear. I often look, without answering, or before answering, I turn the answer over in my head for a long time. I stutter, people laugh at me. And so on.

To give me courage, I secretly hope of returning to Laos, a wish my mother says every day in a single and unique phrase that means everything and nothing:

"When we return to our country...". So I hold on and, with a certain weariness, drag myself to school every day.

The hardest part is staying locked in the same place all day. Finally, I find an ideal solution: to get used to this new life and not suffer from the gaze and contempt of others, I start to develop the art of total detachment and repeat my mother's favorite phrase to myself internally. This is my everyday prayer to be stronger: "When we return to our country, I will be free…" However, time passes, and my hope vanishes quickly. The "country…" seems to have been only an imaginary country or a dream from which one must wake up to move forward.

So I learn to speak by memorizing each word. It is as complicated as learning to write, especially since Hmong writing does not exist and I never went to school "in the country". Mentally, it is quite a story: before making a sentence, each letter is written in my head. I can see the complete spelling at the same time I pronounce each word and each sentence.

I often do not understand what people say to me, and for fear of being ridiculous, I smile. Most Asians display this behavior: it is being reserved but also incomprehension. As for reading, I do not know by what miracle I learned, since my reserve and my shyness never gave me the courage to read a single text in class in my entire life. Even less at home. In fact, I think that for a very long time, no one, not even me, heard the sound of my voice. Some people probably wondered if I could speak.

Over the years, the difference in language diminishes.

*

At school, I also learn songs in German, and the music is easy for me to memorize, I do not know why. What is certain is that I remain unobtrusive, and my teachers stand out through their personalities: they are all-powerful in my eyes through their knowledge. I have a lot of respect, mixed with fear, for them.

There is Mister Julien, a tall and thin man, with long fingers and white hair, always dressed in his blue blouse, so worn that it looks like khaki green. He is strict, but he is a good teacher, and I quickly learned spelling and poetry from him. When a student does something stupid, he is entitled to the donkey cap with him or a slap on the fingers using the ruler. I am entitled to this second punishment, I no longer know the reason, but my fingers still remember it.

Mister Lambert is, it seems to me, my third-grade teacher. He is a handsome man. He has brown hair, and his blouse is a flamboyant new blue. I am a little in love with him, until the day he pulls my ear. That day, a friend decided to ignore the rules by staying in the playground, after the bell rung. I feel obligated to stay with her. Mister Lambert does not appreciate our presence outside, my friend is still sitting on the edge of the window: he pulls my ear and I feel humiliated like never before. So I decide not to pay attention to him anymore.

The principal of the school also teaches fourth/fifth grade. He is a relatively strong man with a round face and square shoulders. He is nice, and I am having a good year in fifth grade. While I am in his class, I have my first medical check-up. Of course, I wonder what the doctor is doing: he examines me, weighs me, asks me to read letters on a sign, letters that are barely visible... I can not see a thing: everything is as blurry as in the classroom!

For several years now, I have been sitting in the front row. I think it is to help me overcome my shyness and to keep a better eye on me or hear me better when I am questioned... But I understand better now, I was seeing blurred. A report was made to my father: "Your daughter urgently needs glasses!" Which means I am as near-sighted as a mole. But my father, very strict, counts the pennies and accuses me of saying anything to the doctor, to make myself interesting and force him to waste money on useless things. So, I get nothing and, on top of that, I get scolded. He keeps the accounts down to the penny, and the money only goes on food.

In fourth grade, a trip was organized to Germany, but I knew my father would not allow me to go because of our poverty. So, when a caring comrade asks me the question:

"And you, aren't you coming?"

I am embarrassed to answer, for once, someone is interested in me.

"I don't know. I don't think so. I have to ask my father."

A few days later, because it took a few days to find the courage to do it, I asked my father, who told me: "No."

That is all. There is nothing to discuss.

So I show my mother a sign of rebellion by telling her my incomprehension and how unfair I find it all. After four years in school, living with the little French people, I am starting to no longer feel like a Hmong.

At the instigation of my classmates and teachers, the parents of the students organized a fundraiser, and I was left with enough money to pay for the trip and even some pocket money. But my father certainly refused. It was hard to understand his motives, and I resented him for a very long time. Years later, however, he finally explained:

"When you're not at home, you're a foreigner! And if you were arrested in Germany, they'd send you back Laos. You wouldn't be so smart, would you?"

Well, the tone is there: I understand that I had a narrow escape, which calms me down quite a bit for other "rebellions" of this kind.

I took my first trip away from the family in elementary school during a snow class in fifth grade. Curiously, I do not have to fight to be allowed to go.

I am even a little afraid to go off alone, but I let myself be carried along by my classmates. It is a sign that I fit in well. They find me a small suitcase for the occasion, but I do not know how to pack. Looking closer, I do not have much to take. My clothes look like rags; I don't remember what color they were. No doubt, very large and very black. As for my shoes, they are sneakers, the only shoes that I can wear for a long time. I have always suffered from foot pain; in Laos, I walked around barefoot, so there was no problem with shoe size.

I am having a fabulous time but feel lonely, even more alone than usual. There is no snow in the snow class, so the teachers keep us busy with field trip. I discover archery and treasure hunting. I am proud to see that I am pretty good at these two activities, which are new to me. Afterward, we go on long hikes and gather in front of a log fire late at night, singing songs that still stay with me: "*on descend de la montagne*[28]" and "*petit garçon*[29]"... Childhood moments are significant moments of life.

Then we went skiing on the grass, but they had trouble finding shoes for me: I have small feet and enormous calves.

I remember how bad I felt for an hour trying on every possible boot with an instructor. Size 40 for calves, 35 for feet. I end up wearing a 38 with two pairs of socks. Needless to say, I look awkward in my oversized ski boots. So as not to frustrate the students, the instructors take us to higher altitudes, where snow is whitening the landscape. With my giant shoes, it is a disaster: I am crowned queen of the fall. In fact, I fall all the time, and I definitely hate the "fun" of sliding.

In the evenings, my roommates write letters

---

28 *She'll Be Coming 'Round the Mountain,* a children's nursery rhyme inspired by the negro spiritual When the Chariot Comes.

29 *Little Toy Trains*, song written by Roger Miller (1967).

summarizing their wonderful stay to their families, especially their moms. I do not know what to say to my mother. I am not going to write that I miss her! And that I spend all my time being afraid of everything! In the end, I send her a card, which she probably would not read because she can not read.

On the last day, it starts to snow, and some people are frustrated not being able to enjoy the beautiful snow falling in abundance, but not me. I am happy to pack my bag for the return trip. We bid a tearful farewell to the friends we had met during our stay. We sing "*Ce n'est qu'un au' revoir*[30]", and sadness grips my throat, even though I have not necessarily made any new friends. It is hard to say goodbye.

As I get off the bus, I impatiently watch for my mother. When suddenly she appears among the crowd of parents kissing their children, dressed in her poorly buttoned floral blouse and her pleated skirt, wearing her scarf, she looks like an alien. But I am happy to see her again and, with my heart racing, I walk towards her, hoping for a hug. Coldly she greets me by saying "Ah, here you are. " and does not even reach out to take my hand.

She immediately turns on her heel and I follow her obediently, like a shadow in pain.

*

As a matter of fact things are not easy for her either.

---

[30] *Till we meet again,* inspired by a scotich song.

Back home, she spent her days working in the fields from morning until night, and she was rarely home. It is the countryside, life in the great outdoors. Forests as far as the eye can see, rivers flowing freely, animals roaming freely. Neighbors and friends with whom to chat, gossip, and laugh. In Castres, she lives locked up in an apartment which, in the long run, seems too small for my father and her.

The embroidery is her only hobby. She is completely out of step with this new life: she dresses randomly, and there is no one who is interested in her. Morally, it is very hard, especially since my father speaks badly to him. She does not hesitate to talk back.

At the same time, they start drinking and often fight under the influence of alcohol. At first, we pay attention to them, trying to separate them, but then we end up letting them roll on the ground, completely disinterested. After a few minutes of melee, they stop, out of breath, this absurdity has calmed their anger.

Sometimes, my mother, like a fury, chases me, screaming, to my room where I take refuge under the bed. To dislodge me, she grabs the broom to chase me away like a repulsive piece of trash: her eyes flash at me with anger. I wonder what I could have done to make her treat me like this.

For a child whose parents represent everything, it remains frightening to see: they are infallible people, gods worthy of admiration who can overcome all difficulties... But they are only human beings trying to be parents in a world that is not theirs. I do not know how they hold on and what they spend most of their time doing when we are at school. However, as the years go by, they miss the country and have a hard time living in exile.

My father is trying to integrate: he is hired in the Renault factory located on the other side of the city. My mother acts as a housewife: her only way out is to pick me up from school. She looks forward to the weekend to go to the market which is located "in town". In the middle of the square sits the statue of the politician Jean Jaurès[31], who was born in this town and gave his name to the square. She wakes me up at seven to go with her. I complain that it is too early, but she argues that it will be too late if we delay. She knows I need at least an hour to be ready...

We walk a long time before we get there. Along the zigzagging sidewalks and the roads that we have to cross, the shame of being foreigners follows me at every step. Beyond this sort of discomfort that I cannot explain, it is the fear of speaking, of stuttering, of being judged.

My mother points to the vegetables and fruits she wants to buy, showing the number of fingers and two words, "one kilo[32]" with a sharp back accent that I laugh at internally. It is mean of me, but my father keeps yelling at her when she goes out with her multicolored scarf tied around her head. It is a tradition that this scarf covers the heads of Hmong women. It is like a second skin or a nearsighted person

---

31 Jean Jaurès (1859-1914): politician and journalist, he created a newspaper "L'Humanité", acting for peace.
32 One kilogramme: about 2.2 pounds

who can not go out without his glasses.

"Aren't you ashamed to go out like that! Stop being such a peasant!" He is ashamed of her and starts saying nasty things to her, and I confess that I am ashamed of going out with her, too. Now that I know a bit more, I think I am smarter. But I think I am largely mistaken. I am a little more educated, but I am a complete idiot.

In town, there is a store on three levels selling pretty things: clothes, scarves, bags, sweets, fruits, and vegetables. In short, all sorts of things that I want to buy, and I like to hang around without buying anything. It allows me to dream a little... The return journey is the same: the relentless sun of the scorching summer burns the skin and gives us a little color that hides our pale yellow.

*

When she wants to blackmail me, my mother hits me with her favorite phrase, thinking that it will have an impact on me:

"When we return to our country…"

It is a sign of her homesickness. She believes in it so strongly that as a result of believing in it with her, I end up despising her for trying to convince me of this impossible return. There is no more hope, and her blackmail can no longer work on me. But she does not want to fail in her role as a mother and wants to teach me the basics of life to become a good daughter-in-law. "Come let me teach you how to embroider."

You'll need it when we return home..."

But I refuse. There is no point in knowing how to embroider today. And I answer her:

"I have homework."

She has no argument to counter: my father is totally on my side. Finally! For him, studying is the most important way to get a good job and avoid poverty. My mother does not want to let me down and insists heavily.

"Come let me teach you how to cook rice. You need to know because when we return to the country..."

So she explains to me the two ways of doing it: you have to let the rice soak for a whole day in a basin. Then, we drain it and put it to steam in a rice steamer until the rice grains begin to soften. We let it soak for a few minutes in water with the drain basket, then we finish steaming it in a few minutes. The other method is simpler: it is the one used by those who forgot to soak their rice. Simply pre-cook the rice in a pan for a few minutes until the grains are soft, then finish steaming.

"Come let me teach you how to crush chili. Dishes are better when you have chili because, when we return to our country..."

You have to put the pepper in a clay pestle, add glutamate and salt, then crush and grind the little red bits, which start to give off such a strong smell that I start coughing until I cry:

"Don't touch your eyes! Chili pepper is spicy!"

But I am completely locked to all that. I do everything to brush aside differences. I do not want anything to do with my origin. I do not want to speak Hmong, especially in public. I am ashamed of being Hmong. I have to fit in, whatever the cost...

Only, I can not take a step without my mother. She asks me to go with her everywhere. In spring, she takes me to collect wild plants that she has spotted not far away. She calls them "zaub iab". It is a weed that grows on piles of dirt. You should pick the tender ends and avoid picking them when the plant has aged too much and is starting to bear fruit. My mother makes a broth from it, which has a bitter taste.

Then there is also a climbing plant that grows in brush or shrubs. It resembles the zucchini plant, with curls and white flowers. You have to take the ends, slice them, and mix them with eggs to cook into an omelet. It tastes nutty. But you should not eat it when it produces black fruits. It becomes toxic.

After that, my mother drags me to the local church every Sunday. At first, people turn away, not without discretion, but make no comment. Mass service is long and insignificant for her and me, but I hear that my father wants to convert because he leaves his shaman altar discreetly behind a curtain. It is my mother who represents him at church to show his willingness to believe in god.

I stay next to her, listen without understanding anything, observe to make the sign of the cross, and when the time comes to "giving peace[33]" to my

---

33 *Giving peace*: before Communion, the priest invites each parishioner to shake hands with his neighbors as a gesture of brotherhood.

neighbor, I am at my worst.

We nod our heads with a little smile, it always works. Then, during the Communion process, we almost always remain alone in our pew, it is curious. We are not entitled to the host, who knows why[34].

It still lasts a few weeks, but it does not seem to please the Good Lord or the Spirits who gravitate around my father. Here, he brings out his gongs, bells, buffalo horns, incense, and red headdress. His Spirits are powerful. They want my father to continue serving them. The practice of shamanism is not easy in a country populated by unbelievers.

By trying to blend into French society, we become uncultivated. I know nothing about French traditions as much as Hmong rituals and traditions. I am even too ashamed to speak Hmong outside the family, and among brothers and sisters, we all speak French. We make little effort in the ancestral rituals, which consist of remembering our dead every New Year by offering them a meal. Or, to sacrifice animals, oxen, pigs, chickens... It is true that the bigger the animal, the more difficult it is to do it in the apartment. Also, the chicken is the animal of choice when it is necessary to make a sacrifice to thank the spirits.

My mother always attends to my father in his ritual. She places the bowl of rice with a raw egg in the middle on the altar, lights the incense, hands him the buffalo horns he throws on the ground to get the answers he is looking for when he is in a trance,

---

[34] Among Catholics, only the baptized are allowed to eat the host, the body of Christ.

and beats the gongs. He speaks in a language made of incomprehensible words or sounds. We can not determine the meaning, but it means he is talking hard with the spirits. Negotiations can last several hours, during which he dances in circles, climbs onto a bench to throw himself off, takes a mouthful of water or alcohol, and spits it around the patient when the latter is present...

It all sounds very complicated, and I am not wrong to say that none of us ever want to have to do it. But it seems that in our family, we have been shamans for generations. Two of my aunts are, and so is my father. If we have to, we will have no choice.

One day, the spirits will choose one of us, the most sensitive and the most receptive, and the chosen one will be obligated to serve them under penalty of inexplicable and incurable illnesses. It is how they have always manifested themselves.

5

My parents keep in touch with the family still in Thailand camp, thanks to recordings on audio cassettes. First, they slip a few bills into the envelope for our sister Choua, whom I have never met. She is the second child in our family, after my brother Guia. When we left Laos, she was already married, but her husband's family did not flee, so she stayed. Unfortunately, her husband was taken prisoner by the Viet Cong and never returned. Choua reached Thailand, following our trail. With no news of her husband, she had to marry another man: it is better to survive together.

Even though she became a mother, her second husband refused to go into exile. The money my parents send her allows her to live without too much difficulty.

Our aunts and uncles wait patiently for their visas for the United States, and news from France is welcome. No one can read or write, so the cassette is used several times. After my mother's tears reach them, my aunts and sister send the tape back to her with their own. We blow our noses, the emotion is palpable. It is so hard to be separated by thousands of kilometers and to think that they will probably never see each other again...

The distress that adults experience in these moments of exile is unimaginable. Then my mother learns that the money does not reach its destination, so she rolls up the notes and puts them inside the cassettes.

One day, it is euphoria. On my way home from school, I learn that my brother Blia, whom everyone thought was dead in the forest, is alive.

How is this possible? It is a miracle!

My father's friends had been asking around for news of a young man with no family who resembled Blia's description and lived in a village. He is married and has a daughter.

It is really him, the proof is finally made. He was sent a coded message informing him that his family is alive and living in France. The day of the fake attack that made us flee into the forest, he thought we were all dead. So he ran as far as possible and hid for days in cemeteries, fearing men more than ghosts. Then, he sided with the "communist" Hmong to save his life.

My parents want him to join us, but it is up to him to make the choice. He would have to leave everything to come alone; otherwise, it would have been impossible. For my brother there is no hesitation: he decides to join us. My father wants to keep his family around him. His great disappointment was not being able to bring our sister Choua, who died a few years later of internal bleeding during pregnancy.

"If she were here, she would be alive!" he said furiously with his son-in-law.

Blia integrates quickly. He and Pheng are courageous young adults. More than anyone else, they know how important it is to find your place in France quickly. Our parents rely on them to educate us and provide for us. Both soon find wives and leave the Tower. Blia went to live with his wife Kia in a small village in the *Montagne Noire*[35], and Pheng moved to the Paris region with his wife Marie and their daughters Caurlhye and Caurnhoue.

My sister Zeu takes care of all the paperwork and transportation, taking us to the Mammouth supermarket on Mazamet Road. What a joy to be able to get out of our neighborhood! In her little orange Peugeot 104, she takes us for walks in the Sidobre, a place where nature has sculpted rocks into different shapes, and then for a picnic by a river, a tributary of the Agoût[36]. The small stream is accessed by a path hidden by foliage. The clear water sings on the stones where crabs hide. We watch with amusement as the small fish swim against the current. It is a peaceful, pleasant place, far from civilization. Only the echo of cars in the distance tells us we are in a free country.

We set off to visit our cousins in Clermont-Ferrand with Zeu, an opportunity for me to discover that I am carsick. To get to the capital of Auvergne, we take endless winding roads. I fill a few bags with vomit, the sight of which makes me even sicker...

Like many Hmong families, my Aunt Gua-Ning and my cousins all live in apartments. It was with them

---

35 Black mountain, situated in the south of France.
36 Agoût : river which flow through Castres.

that we had walked through the forest. But they do not talk about it; why bring back painful memories?

Are we not well like this? We dare a little sightseeing by climbing to the top of Puy-de-Dôme[37], again via a winding road. From there, you dominate all the surroundings, and your gaze is lost on the horizon, between mountains and valleys; it is truly vertiginous. And it reminds us of the mountains of Laos...

---

[37] Situated in the middle of France, the Puy-de-Dôme is a departement which is the name of an extinct volcano.

6

The family gets bigger every year, which makes us less nostalgic. In any case, no one talks about the country anymore, we are all too happy to be reunited. There are now seventeen of us. The firstborn in France brings joy and hope to the older ones. The arrival of other Asians makes us feel less foreign, even if most families live in the "Le Petit Train" district.

As the grown-ups drive, we manage to get together from time to time for gatherings.

Now, we have become part of the landscape, and the locals seem to have adopted us.

In 1984, my parents decided to move to the area where their elder children had left to find work in the Paris region. At first, it was the men who went first. They settle with the family living there first and tirelessly search for a permanent position. They will take any job. All they know how to do is with their hands: so they end up as lathe operators, cab drivers, cement deliverymen, workers in shallot-packing factories, car washers... After this, they find an apartment and return to bring their families. They rent a truck and load it all the way to the top. There is not much to take with them, but the truck can be used to move several families. Those who drive follow in the car with the whole household.

My brother Pheng welcomes us in Draveil, a middle-town in the department Essonne, situated near Paris. There are twelve of us in their small ground-floor apartment in a neighborhood called "Les Bergeries". It is not an ugly place: each building is set on a lawn where pretty trees with large foliage grow. We enter the building one afternoon. It is deserted: no nosy people around. It is so much better: I am afraid of running into neighbors, and it would be terrible to see questioning and judging looks in their eyes.

Two boys sleep in one room, while the living room is cut off by a partition for the third; my sister and I have a room, as do our parents. The young couple and their three children are in one bedroom.

We do not have much to put in place, except for some clothes. In the Paris region, our anonymity saves us from the racism we have often experienced, which we never mentioned. Here, we are barely noticed, especially as we have kept the discretion we learned in Castres for nearly seven years.

The oldest ones took care of all our paperwork. They enrolled us in the nearest school. For me, it is the middle school at the Collège Alphonse Daudet, situated about 1.24 miles from my neighborhood.

You have to go through a narrow alley between houses, hidden from everyone's view. If you do not know the way, you have to take a long detour. Seeing a crowd of teenagers converging on the hedges bordering two houses, I clearly see this alleyway, which saves me a few precious minutes. It leads to a residential area. Following the road, you come to another perpendicular road, which you have to cross to reach the sidewalk of the middle school next to a gymnasium. Together, they face houses.

In the grip of a severe adolescent crisis, something taboo in the family, I am gaining weight on all sides. I wear baggy, loose clothes that make me look like a sumo wrestler to hide my curves. I am being teased by a red-haired, freckled boy. He waits for me almost every morning before the school entrance to insult and shame me. Sometimes, I take a twenty-minute detour behind the school, past the gymnasium, to reach the entrance from the other side. What a pain! But it is better than facing his insults.

One morning, I decide to ride my bike to school. But because I am so small, my feet barely touch the pedals, which I often use standing up. Back for lunch, around a slightly sloping bend, I try to avoid my classmates walking on the road. I went flying and smashed my nose on the low wall of the house opposite. I return to my apartment, bloodied, and my family yells at me. My mother, while caring for me, told me:

"There you are all battered! You who are not beautiful, you are even less so now!"

I started to cry, I needed more compassion... After lunch, I walk back to school with a bandage on my nose, and I do not even get an X-ray to check that nothing is broken. It is already too much nonsense on my part.

My brother Pheng and his wife work hard, and no one has time to care for an insecure teenager. Every morning, I see them leave and come back exhausted at the end of the day. My mother and I look after their little ones. In the evening, we have to cook for twelve people! It is a real challenge. There is no privacy, even if everyone does their best to keep things running smoothly.

There are always people in the shared spaces. You have to form a line outside the windowless bathroom. The dining room is the central room: you pass through it to get to Kou's room and the kitchen, then down the corridor to the bathroom and bedrooms, the only place you can be alone. We often argue here. Living together is not easy. Everyone has their temper: some like peace and quiet more than others. Those who have homework to do cannot stand the music of nostalgic teenagers... Arguments are frequent, and only our parents can settle the dispute by giving us a "*khauj tsiav*[38]".

My father, unable to find a job, gave up driving for good: the roads are narrow, and people drive erratically. It is still the older siblings who drive us.

My sister Zeu has just found a job as a seamstress in a company that makes sofa covers. She excels

---

[38] *Khauj tsiav*, means a tap on the head (with the index and middle fingers bent). It's a painful, humiliating punishment equivalent to spanking. Touching a Hmong's head is a sign of total disrespect.

in this profession. Many Hmong women work in this field. Thanks to this job, she benefits from the 1% employer's contribution and obtains our first apartment at 6 allée du Plateau des Glières, opposite The Bergeries, in the Brossolette neighborhood. It is party time! Life might finally get better. We were really starting to suffocate: how much longer could we live in these conditions?

The new apartment is on the first floor, in the janitor's lodge building. It is a couple in their thirties: the man is tall with brown hair, the woman short and blond. They have a dog, a German shepherd, that I am a little afraid of. We rarely see them: it is just "hello" and "goodbye". It is like that all the time. We stay among ourselves because we do not really know how to behave with others.

The apartment has two bedrooms and a large living-dining room, which the men separate with a partition to make a third bedroom. It is where my sister sleeps; the three boys sleep together and I sleep in my parents' room. There, they make room for a bookcase, desk, bed, and shelf for my clothes. The center of the apartment, the living room, is a place where my father sits to watch TV, and my mother to do her embroidery. She makes bedspreads and pillowcases collected by an association promoting Hmong art.

We do not go out much, either. Our father forbids it. Only during the summer holidays am I allowed to go and play with my brothers behind the building where the ground is tarmacked. We play tennis and badminton. We also subscribe to Club Dorothée[39] and Tex Avery cartoons. It's scrabble, cards, and bickering on rainy days. The narrowness of the small living room makes us nervous: we do not talk much, and we have no topics of conversation. Everyone lives in their own little world.

My father makes sure that everything is in order: taxes, income tax returns, identity papers, social security, and political refugee cards, as well as residence permits. We have to be patient with all the paperwork required by the authorities. We often have to go to the town hall's social assistance department, where my mother and I queue up for the whole family. What a chore! I am always ashamed when we go to see her or queue up at the social services office and, even worse, at the CAF[40] to provide them with proof of our situation. I feel like we are begging! What weakness! What humiliation! Men are smarter to let women line up for this kind of quest.

Once a month, when all the bills are paid, I go with my parents to buy meat at Novoviande on the Nationale 7, in Viry-Châtillon. They buy meat in large quantities: smoked pork bellies, chickens, dry sausages... My mother and I spend a few hours back at the apartment, cutting them up and putting them in plastic bags that my mother keeps from previous freezings. She does not throw anything away. She has missed so much that she saves every plastic bag, every

---

39 Club Dorothée is a show for children, very popular from 1987 to 1997.
40 CAF is a social organism which helps people in need.

piece of fabric, every piece of wire for hypothetical future uses. My father has never worked again, but my mother is starting a home-based job. An industrial sewing machine is installed in the small entrance hall, where a recess is used for storing shoes.

She makes fashion hair accessories. The sewing machine runs until late at night. However, it does not stop; the work has to be finished because the delivery is due the next day. So my father and I get to work, too. To do this, we insert the headband into the cover my mother has just sewn. Sometimes we work until two in the morning.

It gives her an income that she is proud to have.

Velvet, cotton, synthetics, red, black, green, blue threads... scatter their residues throughout the apartment for a long time. My mother increases her efforts for greater earnings since she is paid by the piece and offloads the household chores to me.

Clearing and cleaning the table, washing the dishes, sweeping up... It is late when I settle at my desk, wedged between the parental bed and my mother's drawer. Forced to hand in my homework, which I always do at the last minute, I often fall asleep on my notebooks and textbooks. Even though he is glued to the television, I feel my father's shadow watching me as I wearily blacken my sheet of paper. Words dance before my eyes but pass right through me, leaving no trace or flow over me as if I were waterproof. I can not retain anything and often collapse on the desk.

The following day, seven o'clock is already ringing, and all sleepy, I dress like a robot to catch the bus two blocks away towards the grocery store Intermarché. Sometimes the bus passes without stopping, because it must be late too. I wave my arms uselessly and head back to the apartment, where my father lectures me before a big brother rushes me off to the high school of Montgeron.

Obviously, the high school is closed. I have to go around through the other entrance located on Avenue de la République. The high school, located in a park, is huge. Trees form lines along the paths, muddy in rainy weather and scattered with leaves in autumn. During breaks, I sit with a few friends in a discreet corner to listen to them, telling me their lives made up of unfair things they are victims of, desires to leave the family home, the incomprehension of their needs... I realize how out of step I am with the teenage girls I hang out with. My life is so different: I am very well-behaved, obeying the adults who provide for my basic needs. But do I have desires, dreams, and wishes like them?

I have not thought about it. Like my brothers and sisters, I am like a robot, trying to prove that I deserve to have survived the ordeals we have been through together. You have to succeed in your integration through success, which symbolizes a sort of revenge on fate: I have been conditioned like this since I was a child. And outside the home, I do not want to owe anything to anyone. It is as if I refuse to bind myself to anyone, always ready to leave and remain free of any lasting friendship.

In the evening, the bus takes me back to the apartment, where, at 6:30 pm, my mother and I start preparing dinner. In front of the television, the meals, made of fried meats, meats in broth, and rice, are quickly swallowed, our eyes fixed on the screen. Generally, we do not speak when our eyes are captivated by images, our ears are strained toward loud sounds, and our mouths are full. My father always leaves crumbs and rice between his legs. After each meal, he picks them up when he can, and I sweep up the rest. My mother always sits last, next to my father; perhaps her habit she has kept from our country: being seated when everyone else has already finished eating. This time, I take over. There is always one last thing to bring back from the kitchen, so I am the last one to eat. But do not worry, there are always leftovers. In any case, it is always the meal of the poor, the little people. When you have missed out, it is for the rest of your life - nothing can make up for the void.

7

My sister Zeu has been seeing a man who lives in Grigny for some time. He has already married twice and has five children. She falls in love with him, and as time goes by, a marriage becomes clearer.

He obtains my father's approval and asks his family for a loan, so that he can make a dignified appearance before my parents.

Unfortunately, on the way, he forgets that he has put the money on the roof of his car and only realizes it once he arrives at Cité Brossolette. It is a bit upsetting, but the wedding is happening anyway. My parents are not difficult people. They taught us honesty, respect, and, above all, never to take advantage of the misfortune of others.

She leaves the family home. I think my mother is worried but happy that her daughter has finally found a husband. The rooms are redistributed accordingly. My brother Kou takes the "living room" bedroom. Suddenly, the weight of the family weighs heavily on his shoulders: now he is alone, bringing in an income for the household. It seems impossible for him to provide for the whole family: pay the bills, the rent, the taxes. His salary as a laborer, added to the social assistance benefits, are just enough: the grant pays for clothes and school supplies, the APL[41] pays part of the rent, and the family allowance pays for food.... Life is still just as difficult.

Fortunately, even though they have made a life for themselves, my older siblings are still around. My brother Guia and his family, along with my sister Nadia, live in Tarterêts, a neighborhood that does not have a very good reputation. The shopping center at the heart of the estate is often broken into or vandalized. Residents live in fear as rival gangs form to "wage war" on other run-down neighborhoods in different cities, such as Grigny, Grande Borne, or Evry's Pyramides.

However, families stay in their apartments and do not encounter any significant problems.

My brother Guia has two boys, and my sister Nadia has three boys and a girl. My sister Zeu soon gives birth to a little girl with round cheeks.

They count on the younger ones to get an education so they do not end up like them as laborers. It is so hard to work locked up all day and never complain about your colleagues or superiors, who are sometimes haughty and disrespectful... But they do not ask themselves any question: you have to work to

---

[41] APL: Money help giving by the government for payment of the flat.

provide for your family. So they work, too happy to have the chance to have a job.

Only, in my head, I am ready to work, too. Since studying is hard, I can not see myself studying every night after housework... I am looking forward to my senior year so I can finally turn the page on school. Anyway, I do not know what job I want to do. I cannot sew, I am clumsy with my hands, and the baccalauréat (high school diploma) I have chosen will take me straight into the world of work. It is the secretarial Bac G1. In the final year, the management teacher does not hesitate to tell the girls, pointing to the boys:

"You'll be their secretaries!"

I did not like that sexist remark. And even if it is true, a teacher has to be impartial. I glare at him. But it is no use. Back then, teachers had a bit more power than they do now. No one dared contradict them...

While I am struggling through my last year of high school, my brother Blia buys himself a little house in Savigny-le-Temple, in Seine et Marne. It is a field where many small townhouses have sprung up and where young couples are buying their own homes at rates of around 18%. The town is determined to reduce social inequalities by developing residential areas to offer the middle classes the possibility of becoming homeowners at "low cost". Soccer fields and swimming pools are being built, and green spaces are being developed around water retention ponds where fish are released.

My brother immediately buys a fishing license and

gives it to my father. We finally eat meat other than pork and chicken. My mother quickly taught me how to gut and scale fish. What a chore! Take a very sharp knife, open the fish, empty it of its internal organs... The hardest part is cutting off its head. Not very good at it, I try several times. Poor thing, it's a good thing it is dead!

My two sisters and my brother Pheng also become homeowners. After all, even if mortgage rates are high, why not buy? My father always says: "It's better to have a house, to deprive yourself as long as you can pay your bills. Being a tenant is throwing money out the window! Buy when you can, so they can never kick you out of your home."

At the same time, they bought their houses in Saint-Germain-lès-Corbeil, a town with a somewhat upper middle-class reputation, located on the right bank of the Seine[42], in the heights of Corbeil-Essonnes[43]. Here, too, these are immense fields transformed into residences.

The houses are modern. They even get to choose the tiles on the first floor and the carpets upstairs. These are moments of realization for little peasants from a faraway land to become owners of a little piece of France... The whole family opens up a little more to the outside world. My sister and her husband have a house at the entrance to their neighborhood. They can not choose the location of their house, nor can they buy bigger for their smaller budget. And yet, as fate would

---

42 The Seine, the river which flow through Paris.
43 We all live in Essonne area.

have it, they quickly forged strong friendships with their neighbors, all young parents like themselves. The children attend the same school and start hanging out with the new "bobos[44]" in their neighborhood. It is a new beginning based on a different way of life: tending the garden, having family meals in a large dining room, in summer around a barbecue.

Our parents are proud to see their elders showing the younger ones the way. They are sure that the younger ones will do as the older ones do, that is how things always go, naturally. The new generation would not know the "housing project" like we do.

*

I pass my high school diploma successfully, without distinction, I do not care. My brothers loudly disapprove when I register with the ANPE[45] to work. My father says nothing, but he agrees with his sons. In our family, the older have always educated the youngsters, and especially when you are a girl, they have even more say.

"If we'd known, we'd have forced you to continue," they say reproachfully!

I decided to stop studying without telling them. Anyway, it is too late! I have already got my first job as a temp.

They did not insist since I was the first to graduate. Having repeated a year, my brother Zo will not be

---

44 Bobos, meaning "new richmen".
45 National job center.

taking his high school diploma until next year. He and Yen decided to study and did not disappoint our father.

Good, because I am finally enjoying my freedom. I quickly realize that you cannot do much with a high school diploma. So I decide to take a training course: you study in the adult world and what is more, you are paid by the government!

I will be twenty in a few days, and I plan to celebrate with a nice meal, now that I have my own salary. With sister Zeu's help, we are buying all the ingredients a week before the meal, as we will be celebrating my birthday at her place. After the shopping, my father is letting me sleep at my sister's. I can not believe it!...

But it was too good to be true: as usual, at the last minute, he changes his mind and sends my brother Kou to fetch me. It is eight o'clock in the evening.

My sister and I cook egg rolls for dinner, a dish that everyone enjoys. After swallowing a few quickly, my brother-in-law and two of his children leave for Grigny in his beautiful red sports car. I can see that my sister is not too happy to see him go: once again, she will be spending the evening alone. Ten minutes later, we hear the ambulance's sirens, then my brother arrives and we take the road to Corbeil.

The phone rings for a long time at night, like in a dream, and it cannot wake me from sleep. But when I hear my brother Kou crying, I am startled and realize that something terrible has happened. My brother-in-law Deng died in a car accident a few yards from my sister's house on the other road, the one that leads to the Francilienne, the same road we should have taken to get back to Draveil; the ambulance sirens were for him... He lost control of his car as the road descended, colliding with a car coming from the opposite direction and crashing into the low wall. He had to be extricated... The details are chilling and mortifying to the core. The children are alive, but one of them is seriously injured. We are devastated and shocked by this sudden, violent death. The world is crumbling around us.

This is our first death here, and it brings us back to the difficult reality of life. We are nothing, and we can lose everything overnight.

The funeral took place in the house he was so proud to own. His coffin is laid out by the dining room window, facing the garden. The house is full of people. People talk, accuse the widow of not having been able to hold him back, tell each other about the accident, cry... My sister, a thirty-year-old widow, remains dignified, but everyone wonders about her future. When a Hmong woman is married, she belongs to her husband's family... What are we going to do with her? Should she sell the house and move elsewhere? But with whom? How to live after this tragedy?

My sister is a courageous woman. As she married a man from the Vang clan, traditionally, the Vang family should offer her a husband from their clan. But they do not have anyone, and it would not be possible for my sister anyway. This tradition cannot continue in France. How does one become the wife of a brother-in-law? It is unimaginable. She decides to continue living in the house. The family is next door if needed, and the neighbors are exceptionally supportive. To keep her company, after the funeral, my parents order me to go and live with her.

The cold and silence settle between us once the house has been emptied of funeral guests. My sister and I sleep in the other room close together at night, and it is hard for me to get up to go to the bathroom at night. Every place is filled with the presence of my brother-in-law... Between irrational fear and lack, we cling to each other like two bruised and frightened little sparrows.

Spring brings back the beautiful days, and the many flowers he planted as soon as he arrived in this house display their petals in an explosion of a thousand colors, and we shed bitter tears of sadness.

*

At the Draveil apartment, things are slowly changing. My brother Kou starts dating a young girl who lives in Rennes. He goes back and forth every weekend before finally asking her to marry him.

She moved to Draveil. I do not know how the rooms are distributed again. Soon, she gives birth to a son. The space is getting smaller as my mother, having grown older, is becoming a bit touchy. And then, the cohabitation between mother-in-law and daughter-in-law has never been a good match... Eventually, they found an apartment in Evry, where they raised their four boys before buying their own house, like the eldest.

My sister and I are establishing a life routine between women: my sister continues to work, my niece goes to school, and I am still in training. The classroom comprises adults who want to become professionals or retrain. In the classroom I meet a young woman who lives in Paris with her boyfriend. We become friends, and they invite me to spend a weekend in Normandy.

I discover the sea for the first time at twenty one, or rather the ocean, and sleep far from my family. It is a new life that is beginning, a new expression that has become part of my language and that I use once a year: going on vacation. I wonder if any member of my family knows what that means.

Since our arrival, we have never been on vacation but have been on many outings with the kids. The parents have always saved, and the older ones have done the same. When one has suffered so much from misery, one cannot allow oneself a moment of relaxation: you keep saving, in case of hard times. You can lose everything so quickly, so to limit expenses, the oldest take us on picnics around the Savigny-le-Temple lake; near the lake, a municipal swimming pool is being built, and next to it, there is a little wood where we go to pick daffodils and lilies of the valley.

We set off in five or six cars filled with children of roughly the same age. The Bréviandes forest is also our favorite place: we can grill meat on barbecues specially installed by the city..

Coal, marinated meats, and rice are transported there and kept warm in coolers. Children and men gather sticks to start the fire. It is the only time when the men are at the stove. The women set the tables. The space is monopolized, and latecomers look at us skeptically. The "Forêt de Fontainebleau[46]" is also our place for a walk: we take our blankets, our rugs, our folding chairs, the rice, the chicken cooked in water, the chili pepper...

Few of us have the luxury of going away in the summer. So, one year, my sister Zeu and I decided to take our parents to see the sea for the first time in their lives. We are going to Arcachon in a small apartment that I have already rented last year. It is located opposite the port. My niece Pama is on the trip. She is a real chatterbox, a little joker, who livens up our stay. A few visits, a trip out to sea, some Italian-style ice cream, lots of walking... My father spices up the trip by having a gout attack. His feet are swollen: they look like two jellyfish without their tentacles. We had to run to the doctor, and my father had to end the vacation locked up in the apartment while we went off to visit Dune du Pilat[47].

We take a few photographs, including a memorable one of my parents, dressed, standing in knee-deep water, hit by an Atlantic wave. A memory I would

---

46 Fontainebleau forest is a big forest in the South of Paris. It is the lungs of Paris area. It is famous because of its various landscape, especially known as a training ground for rock climbers, thanks to its many rocks dating back 500,000 years.

47 Dune de Pilat: is the highest dune in europe, naturally formed, situated in the South West of France, near Arcachon.

have liked to create more often… But when you are a child, you let your picture be taken, and when you are an adult, you are almost ashamed to pose next to them.

8

1991. Our parents are starting to age: my father is 62, and my mother is 56. But they look older. For almost half a century, they have worn themselves out taking their nine children from a country where peasants live as if in the Middle Ages to a modern country, then integrating them into this industrial world where they feel totally on the margins. They can not find anything to give them the illusion of a possible return.

After all these years, they still pretend they do not understand French: in reality, I suspect they are just pretending in order to better solicit us, a way of requesting our presence. My father often replies, "I don't understand, I don't speak French". But perhaps he understands better than we do: he spends most of his time watching television.

The Tour de France[48] with live commentary, soccer matches, the Roland Garros or Wimbledon tournaments[49].

---

[48] France Tour: a cycling competition around France.
[49] Roland Garros (France) and Wimbledon (Great-Britain): Tennis tournaments.

He does not miss the news on TF1[50], neither the political debates that would make anyone cringe.

Now, things are reversed: parents become children, and children become parents. Maybe it is normal after all. They depend on us for everything: visits to the doctor, blood tests, the supermarket... For the trifecta, my father puts on his little grey raincoat and continues along the sidewalk of Avenue Henri Barbusse to the tobacco shop in the small shopping center opposite the Hôpital Dupuytren.

As for my mother, she also has her little ritual: she goes to Intermarché to buy a few trivial things to get out of the four walls of the apartment. She still panics when there is a change in the shelves because she no longer recognizes the prices of the products, which are separated from their packaging colors and location. For a hundred francs[51], we fill the cart with things my father calls useless. But my mother needs to stock up so we do not run out. They move little and eat a lot of "junk foods," candies, very sweets.

They have never deprived themselves of these delicacies since we arrived in France, so, like a sneaky beast, diabetes silently settles into my mother's bloodstream. She has to check her blood sugar level three times a day: she sticks a special needle into the tip of her finger and collects a drop of blood using a strip.

It is placed into a blood glucose meter, which takes the measurement. We write everything down in

---

50 TF1: France principal information channel.
51 Francs: French old money, used before euros.

a notebook to show the doctor that we are taking our monitoring seriously. Depending on the result, she deprives herself of more or less sweet foods.

But it was impossible for her to deprive herself of rice, and yet she would have to.

At this stage of the disease, she takes pills and can still get around without depending on insulin. But depriving herself of everything is difficult, and the disease takes over: now she is entitled to insulin. The injection is subcutaneous; the belly has the most suitable layer of fat to receive the injection, which my mother refuses to give herself. Back at home, after a year with my sister, I am automatically designated. It is not difficult, and I wonder whether I would be able to give myself such an injection...

My father can not leave my mother sick on her own, he also gets involved: he suffers from renal colic and ends up in hospital in Juvisy. He proudly shows us the stones that have come out of his kidneys: as big as a marble, black as coal. He keeps them in the bottle the doctor gave him as if to exorcise a spell cast on him by an evil spirit. In Laos, in our area, which is far away now, it seems that people are capable of "throwing stone[52]" at a person they do not like.

Then, he continues with a stomach problem. Weakened by alcohol abuse, the doctors forbid him to consume even pepper... They have two cupboards full of all kinds of medicines, and consumption must be around a handful per dose.

---

52 *Tso pob zeb,* meaning "throwing a stone", casting a spell on someone.

Weakened by illness, they are counting on my return to Brossolette to care for them. But, after a year of freedom with my sister, it is hard to get back into the family. At nearly twenty-three, I finally got my own room, the one at the end of the living room where almost all my siblings had stayed. It did not take long for the little room to feel like a prison, where I dreamed of being a little bird and flying away as I gazed out of the window...

I convince my father to let me go to Great Britain to learn English. Severe but up to date with all the news, he knows that speaking English would open doors to my professional future. As for my mother, she would like to keep me close to her in these difficult times when illness is increasingly present.

"If you go away," she says, "who's going to take care of giving me injections?"

She can not inject herself, and I understand; I know that for the first time in my life, I am showing shameful selfishness.

To my great surprise, my father is the sole candidate. Watching his trembling hand as I teach him to put the insulin in the needle and prick my mother's belly, I feel guilt gripping my heart. But, for me, too, it is hard to stay.

So I left for London, where I experienced a new exile, but this time, it was voluntary. It changes many things: a voluntary departure or a forced departure. In the first case, it is an assumed choice, and in the second case, it is an imposed choice with no hope of return.

The stakes are not the same. I feel very foreign again, but also very alone. I suddenly understand what family spirit means. Being alone has no meaning for a Hmong, who must live surrounded by family and take into account the judgment of the community.

Yet, back in France, I do not want to fall into line by returning to the bedroom at the back of the living room, which, during my absence, was occupied by Zo. When you leave your parents and the family environment you grew up in, it is very complicated to come back. My decision to live with my sister Zeu disappointed everyone. Nobody understands me: a child must be married to have the right to leave the family. So, my decision is controversial, but my mother stands up to defend my choice for the first time in her life. I look at her, crying and saying: "Thank you, *kuv niam*[53]. You see, your voice can be heard."

I understand at that moment the love she has for me. And the long years of silence, of never speaking out to defend myself, no longer matter to me. I know I have disappointed her a lot and even broken her heart. But it is clear that I am abandoning her as she begins to age and the disease worsens.

Can I find happiness and my path with my parents in my care? I do not feel able to help them the way our elders helped us. I think Western life has made me too selfish.

So, I am moving in with my sister Zeu, as a single girl, to live between girls. To ease my guilt, I travel miles every weekend between Saint-Germain-lès-

---

53 *Kuv niam*, meaning "*maman*"

Corbeil and Draveil to meet their demands: doctors, specialists, paperwork, medical examination...

It makes me feel useful, at the same time as it makes me feel freer in my movements, even if I have to constantly continue to be accountable to my parents at twenty-six years old.

*

It is my brother Zo's turn to fall in love. He meets a young girl from the Moua clan at the Cora hypermarket, where he works as a sales assistant in the computer department. I am designated as "*niam tais ntsuab*[54]". It means I am her chaperone throughout the marriage proposal ceremony, which takes place at her parents' home in Brunoy. It is extremely difficult for me, as I hate sleeping anywhere but in my own bed.

During the negotiations, the future groom and his escorts have to drink several glasses of alcohol, promising to honor their promises to take care of the bride. Zo, who cannot tolerate alcohol, is completely asleep in the car and sprays the toilet with the contents of his stomach as soon as he gets back home. They move into the apartment for a few months before moving to Evry.

They have five sons, the first of whom died of a birth defect..

---

54 *Niam tais ntsuab*, meaning chaperon. See section "The wedding" for explaination about this ritual.

9

After years of waiting in refugee camps in Thailand, my father's sisters, cousins, nieces and nephews have been granted visas for the United States. They live an easier life than we do. The Americans do not talk about integration but assimilation. The Hmong are also recognized as Vietnam War veterans. Older Hmong receive pensions from the army, and commemorations are held every year to honor the end of the war. Hmong Americans hold high positions in public administration and become doctors, lawyers, and heads of big companies...

My parents, tired of seeing me alone, send me to spend a few weeks with my aunts in Minnesota, in the secret hope of finding a husband. I am already an old maid since the average girl has to be married by her twentieth birthday. I am probably starting to embarrass them... Anyway, my brother Blia is my bodyguard.

He forbids me from going anywhere: I have to stay with my cousin and am not allowed to go anywhere unaccompanied. It is a scorching summer in Minneapolis; the outside is heavy with heat and the inside is too air-conditioned. I meet my aunts, who are adorable. But America has not won me over, and I spend my time bored and feeding mosquitoes.

What is more, I have no suitors. Anyway, in France, I began to see a young man I met at the drama class I enrolled in to combat my pathological shyness.

He is Italian, the son of a Sicilian and a woman who was born in Paris. His name is Jean-Giuseppe, but everyone calls him Joseph. I have never been able to integrate into the Hmong community, so my family is not very surprised.

Working and living in freedom allows me to let loose. I say to myself, "nothing ventured, nothing gained," and "you have to set yourself little challenges to learn to overcome your fears," and then "ridicule doesn't kill." Therefore, I discover my talents as a philosopher, psychologist and adventurer who is not afraid to take on the world.

My pen pal becomes my date, lover, and then spouse. But before we settle down together, it is essential to go through an elaborate formal marriage proposal. My parents do not want to complicate the proposal. I am already twenty-seven, considered an old maid, and on top of that, I am marrying a stranger to the community.

We proceed step by step in order to follow some kind of protocol: a formal marriage proposal, within the rules of what is acceptable. We rent a small apartment on the top floor of a building bordering the Essonne in Corbeil-Essonnes. We are entitled to a small piece of the garden for a vegetable patch. My future husband lives there until the pseudo-marriage proposal, which we stage with the blessing of my family.

All my big family gathers at my brother Pheng's house. My future husband is under a lot of stress: he is getting married to a girl from a large family, he is an only child, and what is more, she belongs to a community with a very complicated wedding ceremony.

When my future husband's family and I arrived at the house, it is a huge shock for his parents: there are people everywhere! On the stairs, in the kitchen, in the garden, in the living room... We greet each other, then settle the guests on the living room sofa around the coffee table. Then, there is total silence. Tension mounts for the groom when suddenly someone says something about cats being eaten by Asians. The groom grits his teeth as he realizes it is his mother who has been talking. But the next moment, everyone bursts into laughter, which lightens the mood for good.

Things go pretty well: the wedding delegates keep things simple, and at the end of the day, I am officially married! We head back home to Corbeil, and before we walk in the door, Joseph tries to do like in a romantic series by making me cross the threshold in his arms.

Big mistake! I have put on a lot of weight since England... So we throw ourselves on the sofa under the tender gaze of his parents.

Finally free from our respective families, we enjoy our cozy nest and learn to live together without difficulty.

It is an experience that we enjoy but which, for me, cannot last: I dream of becoming a mother and, like my mother, of having many children, at least four! I realize that I am conditioned by the women in the family, and I can not see my life any other way. Life would be so sad without children...

Two years later, we bought our first house, and in my thirties I become the mother of a lively, adorable little girl, followed by another with round eyes and curly hair, and then a little doll with silky hair. I now understand what it means to be "dependent on your parents".

We no longer have to worry about anything other than ourselves, but our worries are multiplied by the number of people in the family... My mother suddenly has the makings of an outstanding mother, fifteen times more, since there were thirteen children..

10

Our little brother Yen has just finished school. He gets married and becomes dad very soon. His baby's name is Alicia.

He follows the elder's path: buy a house at Moissy-Cramayel to live with the parents[55].

After over thirty years in their apartment in Brossolette, they finally leave Draveil. But all these years mark the old age of our parents and time passing. When they move in with their youngest son, they no longer live in their home but at Yen's place. It changes a lot of things: it is a new stage, the beginning of an inevitable decline where parents become children in our care...

We realize our parents' secret dream of living five kilometers away. Only Zo and his family have moved thirty kilometers farest.

However, we remain united in the face of illness. My mother's diabete makes her totally dependent on hospitals, and she regularly stays at the Louise Michel Hospital in Evry, where she ends up on dialysis. The brain gets used to the worst things when it experiences

---

[55] In Hmong tradition, parents stay with the youngest son.

even the most traumatic situations more than twice. At the beginning of his hospitalization, there was great panic among our siblings.

The family got together to make the right decisions: what to do? Accept dialysis. Manage daily life with home care and hospital visits. Who is in charge?

Everyone contributes in their own way and to the extent of their availability. My brother Blia spends the most time with our parents. He and his wife were diagnosed with kidney failure a few years ago. He takes advantage of his free time to take them shopping or fishing with our father... He recently received a transplant and is starting to make big travel plans. He is going back to Laos to visit the country...

However, my mother is back in hospital and we are worried again. Her hair is all white, and her skin is wrinkled suddenly. She stayed in the hospital for so long that she occupied all the rooms on the dialysis floor...

One night, the phone rings, and my heart leaps into my chest. All the darkest thoughts invade my brain in a matter of seconds.

In the receiver, the voice of my brother Pheng:
"Blia is dead".

I do not understand. I do not want to believe it. I tell myself it is a nightmare.

But it is true. When the morning fog clears, I join my family at the Melun morgue. His aorta had ruptured. There was nothing more to be done, it was too late.

To spare my poor mother any emotional shock, the doctors recommend we keep the news of her son's death a secret. They ask us to make a superhuman effort, so much so that to avoid having to lie, some of us prefer not to go and see her.

My sisters and I are crying quietly in the corridor when she asks about our brother, who came to visit her every day. My mother suspects that something serious has happened and asks us with a sigh:

"Why Blia doesn't come to see me anymore? I have not heard from him for a long time... Tell him to come and see me."

Her face darkens. We hide our eyes to prevent her from reading our dismay. The funeral took place without her in a darkened function room. My father is mortified by grief. He says nothing and wanders like a lost soul from room to room under the endless incantations and tearful cries of the mourners who never finish. For three days and nights, we live this waking nightmare, our heads heavy with sleep deprivation, our eyes puffy with tears, our hearts swollen with sadness, our ears filled with the death drums, our bodies trembling with suffering...

After the burial, we visit our mother as if nothing has happened, and when we tell her the sad news, she remains silent. She stopps speaking to us to make us understand that she is angry with us for having kept everything from her.

*

We try to get on with our lives, but the funeral and instrumental songs ring in my ears for months. It has to be this way for everyone.

Suddenly, everyone becomes aware of the time running towards the inevitable.

However, we do not talk much about our feelings. It is frowned upon to show them; it is a sign of weakness, especially in men. While women embrace for a long time while sniffing at every encounter, men remain closed-faced and stiff-bodied, showing no emotion. Besides, I do not think I saw my father cry.

Blia's funeral was very difficult for him, even if he did not let it show. What could be more terrible for a parent than to lose a child? The ceremony is not perfect: there is a lot of tension. You have to sacrifice an animal, cut it up, store it, cook it for several days... And on top of that, many Elders have died and this kind of tradition is becoming difficult to maintain because the new generation does not want to go through all these heavy and tedious rituals. That is why my father decided to convert to Catholicism. In 2009, he begins the chaplaincy. However, his spirits do not seem to want to let him convert. Soon, his health declined, and his physique changed.

In August, he is hospitalized in Melun for more than two weeks for a liver problem that had grown considerably in size. In the Moissy-Cramayel house, he can no longer go upstairs to his room. We set up a bed for him in the living room, where he sleeps until he can return to his room.

Illness makes parents more vulnerable and fragile,

so I suddenly feel more grown-up than usual. I even find myself lecturing him:

"You need to take a walk. Stop staying in front of the television all the time."

"Your father and Alicia fight every day over who watches television, my mother adds!" He tells me proudly:

"I miss my bed so much that the other day, I made a huge effort! Step by step, I crawled to the top. When I saw my bed, I was so happy!"

He hopes to return one day, as sleeping in the living room is not easy. Unfortunately, as with any older person, when the decline occurs, the fall is precipitous. In October, he is hospitalized again. When I tell him I am going on vacation this All Saints' Day, he says reproachfully, "Why do you have to go?".

I wonder why he always has to make me feel guilty; nothing can happen to him. But deep down, I fear the worst.

As everything is booked, I can not cancel this week's vacation, which we have been looking forward to for so long. Our small budget does not allow us to book in August, so when the offer to rent an apartment in Normandy comes up, I jump at the chance, even though I know we will not be able to go swimming. I try to reassure him, but I am the one I want to convince. I really do not see my parents aging: they are the same as when I left them to live my own life. They were still independent, aging well, and barely had any white hair.

"Go away then! Maybe when you come back, I'll

already be dead!"

"But Dad, you're not going to die!"

I leave with a heavy heart: I wish he had told me:

"Yes, go ahead. You deserve this vacation. It will do you good. Everything will be fine for me."

But in the family, there is a lot of emotional blackmail.

A week later, he is still in hospital, in the same room. He seems to be doing better.

"Ah, there you are," he says.

It feels like a reproach. I blame myself a little, even if I am relieved to find him back to his old self, not very talkative. We exchange small talk, as usual. He tells me he is going to be discharged soon.

The return is not easy. Caught up in my daily routine and knowing that he was in good hands, I did not see him again until a few weeks later. The change is radical: he only gets around with a walker. He no longer recognizes me: when I happen to look into his eyes, I see astonishment in his eyes. Who am I to him? I feel compelled to remind him of this:

"I'm your daughter Maiv."

Then, I help him as he goes to the bathroom and wait for him to finish before taking him back to bed.

It is a difficult time for my younger brother and his wife. I experience all this from afar, vicariously, caught up in my own struggle as a mother of three young children and a working woman.

In December, he fells into a deep coma while my mother was still in the hospital. We travel between Evry and Servon where he was transferred to a medical center specializing for people in comas. During this period, fear isolates me in a parallel world where I have no awareness of the gravity of the situation. I think we are all in this state of unconsciousness.

At the same time, our mother is hospitalized again. But this time, we can not hide our father's situation from her. We get permission to discharge her. On the road, I look at her tenderly: sitting on the bench seat, one hand on the seat belt, as she usually does, she says nothing. It is like a little girl being taken for a walk and looking at the road, patiently waiting for the car to stop. However, this is not for a walk, and she knows it.

What is she thinking about? I wish I knew how to console her. She is so unflappable... When we arrive in the resuscitation room, my father is hooked up to a machine that helps him breathe. All his limbs are swollen, as is his face.

Feverish, diminished, her cane in hand, trembling, my mother approaches my father and whispers a few words. Can he hear her?

"*Kov txiv*, it's time to say goodbye..."

And she starts to cry: it is the first time I have seen my mother cry. She looks so fragile, so alone. After more than sixty years together, how can we say goodbye?

She is so fragile that we quickly bring her back to Evry.

The doctors are unable to tell us the truth about our father's condition. They make us believe in a return home that will require preparation: transfer to a medical home, use of a wheelchair, and mandatory presence of a family member...

My aunts, who have just arrived from the United States, are more realistic and do not delude us. They have already seen many cases like my father. You have to expect that he would not wake up.

The priest comes to bless him in his bed, but he cannot receive baptism in this state...

Our collective unconsciousness deprives us of our father's last moments: we do not understand that it is almost over. Everyone has gone back to work, and our eldest brother is responsible for keeping him company.

As for me, I make a point of going there after work. One evening, I met a cousin who had come to see my father. He says to me:

"They've pulled the plug on your father, I don't know why."

The nurse explains that my father will wake up and that I need to talk to him.

So, even though we never spoke, I told my father about my day and described the snow that was falling in abundance. I hold his hand: it is warm. His breath gently lifts his chest. It comforts me and I tell him that I will come back the next day.

But the next day, snow covered all the roads, and neither my brother nor I had the courage to face the storm. That night, my father decided to leave us.

We have nothing but regrets about that cursed day. Why didn't I go? Why did it snow so hard that night?

Why? Why?

The questions remain unanswered.

My father's funeral takes place in a large hall located in a field in Seine et Marne. We stays up for three days and nights with a parade of compassionate people from all over France. My aunts insist that we sit in front of his coffin; it is torture for me. I cannot accept that in this wooden chest, which we have carefully chosen, lies the body of my father! My brothers and sisters come and go. I can not move from my seat, forced by my aunts, who hold my hand, and I close my eyes so as not to look at the coffin. In the week leading up to the ceremony, I spent many hours looking at photos to make a slide show of my father's life: severe, smiling, absent... His many faces flash before my eyes, while his body is cold and lifeless.

There are no gongs or traditional chants to guide his spirit to his ancestors, only Christian religious songs in the Hmong language.

On the third day, a heart-rending scream is heard in the hall. It is Auntie Kab. She is also a shaman, and she explains that my father's spirit does not know where to turn, since the road to his ancestors is closed, due to the priest's blessing. His spirits do not know how to lead him...

It is a huge shock for me. I start crying with her. Her vision of things shakes me to the core. Have I started to believe in the existence of spirits, too, contradictory to what I think?

Every Hmong, when dying, returns to the valley of his ancestors to spend happy days there... except my father! I imagine him, blocked on his way, without the possibility of passing. My aunt's cry of pain is unbearable.

On the evening of the third day, all that remained were the family and friends; the guests had all left. The room is empty and cold. A small fire is made outside to burn the paper offerings, symbols of money, to allow my father's spirit to pay for his journey to the afterlife. Before going to bed for the last hours with the deceased, we tidy and clean the room, hoping to shorten the night. Even with only a few hours' sleep, this night seems to last an eternity.

The next morning, we barely speak. Breakfast is quick. We can not wait to leave this place that has seen us cry endlessly. When the hearse arrives, we give it a final sweep, pick up the last belongings; we must not forget anything, we must leave without looking back, as if a single glance back would forever inscribe the fateful hours of this "place of misfortune" in our memories. A long procession of cars follows the lead car towards the church in Moissy, where our closest and most faithful friends are already waiting for us.

The church is full. We are seated in the front rows, and the coffin is placed in front of the altar. Our eyes are puffy, but it is not over. The end of this nightmarish film ends at the Moissy cemetery. We all gather around the hole for a final prayer and a song that tears my heart out. The worst moment is the lowering of the coffin. My pain explodes. My heart seems to jump from my chest. I never think I could cry so much and is so painfull.

I lean on my little brother, shouting, "We don't have our dad anymore!" and receive the inexpressive stare of a man who has never known how to express his own feelings.

"We still have Mom, he replies by way of comfort."But that does not comfort me at all.

You have to live "after" my father, alone. When you can not sleep at night and try to forget the images, then the drumming chants. You have to resume the daily routine you left on hold. Getting up in the morning, going to work, facing other people's stares, their embarrassment... Eating and continuing your activities without forgetting the children. Everything is so different and yet so identical to before.

Day after day, the pain is less severe, even if the memories remain anchored.

11

At the Moissy house, silence has settled in. The faces darken, the gazes absent. My mother drags her sick body back and forth between the hospital and her room, where she now sleeps alone. She is scared and has trouble sleeping. Little by little, she declines. Some days, she is delirious about people coming into her room to rummage through her closet. She discreetly hides a machete under her pillow to defend herself, but we replace it with a wooden one. She scatters corn kernels all over the room to drive away evil spirits. It is possible that the large number of medications she is taking are altering her vision of things and that she is confusing days and people. Sometimes, she complains that people have come to take her jewelry or when others keep bothering him by talking loudly... She claims they are ghosts.

We are especially worried about the nurse who comes every morning and evening to give her care and insulin injections.

She often tells us:

"I don't want to leave you."

So, she holds on despite the suffering. She still has all her mind and all her memories, it is just her body that is failing. Eventually, they ended up taking away her big bed and installing a medical bed. She eats very little and can no longer go downstairs to the living room. A small refrigerator and kettle are placed in her room, along with small water bottles.

To get around, she uses my father's walker. Soon she can not even stand up, so we put her in a diaper, which I change for her at midday. She often moans in pain and fidgets around, fully aware of her condition. The pain is like thousands of needles cutting into her, tyrannizing her... Then, it is gangrene on her thumb. It is not a pretty sight. The doctors recommend amputating it, and she shows me her sore thumb and says:

"I love my thumb so much. What can I do next?"

Things get worse and worse. She blames us for not coming to see her enough, even though there is someone with her every day at the house in Moissy, where my brother and sister-in-law leave her to go to work. But that is not enough for her.

"I could just stop eating and die," she says as a final way out of her suffering...

Yet she often says lately: "I'm afraid to die." Who wouldn't be?

For several days now, her infection has worsened. My brother Guia decided to take her to the emergency room of the Sud-Francilien hospital. He waits with her in the corridors for a long time but leaves her alone. For long moments, she faces her loneliness and pain before my sister Zeu comes to take over. When my sister arrives at the emergency room, my mother does not complain. She greets my sister with an icy coldness. She says nothing, as usual, her face closed. She is very angry with everyone because she feels abandoned by her children. Her silence shows her disappointment and a kind of punishment she inflicts on us.

*

When the day of the last farewell comes, everything is jostling in my head, clouded with a thousand useless thoughts, a thousand unanswered questions, a thousand revolts, a thousand billion refusals of the fateful moment. I would like to have a remote control to go back in time, to freeze the moment in an instant, that of childhood, of innocence, of carelessness where we believe that our parents are eternal and will never leave us. I want to scream with all my might, with all my soul, with all my guts, my refusal to let this terrible moment happen. I want to cry, to lose my memory, to die before anyone else, never to know this pain that will never subside and is only growing inside me...

I have settled into a makeshift bed with my sisters, next to my mother. There is also my older sister-in-inlaw. In the small hospital room, we whisper about everything and nothing. We have to kill the silence.

Then night slowly envelops us.

Outside, the road experiences the eternal upheavals of an ordinary night that resembles all other nights. However, for us, it is the beginning of an endless night... I dread this night, listening to every sound and my mother's breathing, which testifies that life is still here. For a moment, I get scared. What if... what if... she died tonight? Will I be able to bear to find her lifeless when I wake up if I fall asleep? I bend my ear to hear her breathing. I am relieved. "No, she's not going to die just yet." When? How many days do we have to watch over her? The doctors have stopped the dialysis. It is only a matter of days or hours. My aching brain pushes this information aside. We do not say anything, but deep down, we know: we watch over her last moments.

The day before, each of her children had come to whisper a few words in her ear, some had stayed alone with her to confide in her one last time. Words against evils: we free her from this life of suffering. "Our children are grown, we have a roof over our heads, we have a family. Now you are free to go... don't worry, don't worry about us..."

I could not say anything. The words had been dead for a long time, choked by two large lumps that clung to my throat. I opened my mouth, and nothing came out except for a ridiculous sentence:

"It's me Maiv, I'm here too!"

I could have said something like:

"My mother, it's me, your Maiv. Forgive me for not living up to your expectations! For disappointing you so often! Even if I'm stubborn, you're my mother, and I love you. I don't want you to leave me. I still need you, Mother."

And I would have started to cry... In front of her, showing her my great weakness, giving her one last remorse for leaving us. When the moment of the last farewell came, I was left with my fear of recognizing this great weakness or the shame of having to say these things that I am not used to saying. Stupidity, pride, or arrogance. It is a pity, it would have taught me humility... and given me the strength to get through difficult times.

When it is time for our final farewell, there are four of us in the room, with my mother, but each of us is alone. Alone in her own thoughts. The television is broadcasting a program of no interest. The night is long, endless.

Beds creak when you turn over to stretch the side where your weight is resting. We do not dare move too much for fear of kicking our bedmate in the face. We lie head to toe in an uncomfortable position, but no one complains. From time to time, we can not hear my mother breathe. However, it is just that she seems to draw a breath from the depths of her lungs that ends exhausted on her lips.

My sister Nadia wets her lips... from time to time. Her chest rises in a rhythmic movement: she seems calm and less tortured, as the day slowly dawns. With it, it seems as if the fog dissipates, that our lives, suspended on the wings of night, suddenly find a renewal that resembles hope. O blessed day! How can you take away so many dark fears from me with a single ray of your light! And immerse myself in a hope so illusory that I am almost ashamed of having believed in you so much!

Everyone decides to go home to shower and wash

up. My brother Guia takes over, and I am next. The early morning drive home dispels the doubt and anxiety of the night. You find yourself believing that all is well, that nothing worse can happen today. However, on my return, at the top of the road called Francilienne, a dark cloud hangs over the hospital. Coincidence or omen?

I reach the parking lot with a heavy heart, get out of the car, and barely enter the hospital lobby before a torrential rain pours down on the building. I meet my brother Guia, who announces to me, without mincing words: "Haven't you heard? She's gone." It is silly, but I didn't understand. "What? Gone? When did she leave? Why?". "She wanted to drink. I gave her some water, then she sighed, and that was it. A tear rolled down the corner of her eye..." He tells us later.

She is lying on the bed where we left her. I dare touch her face? Or her arm? Or her hand? I can not remember. We cry. Someone lets out a heartbreaking complaint. We do not know what to do, we wait for the others. She is still warm. We must dress her before it is too late, before... But it is as if she is asleep, as if she could wake up at any moment. I do not want to believe, I am afraid to believe...

When the final farewell is announced, you would like to be deaf to hear nothing and blind to see nothing.

The human brain is ambiguous: my mother, by dying, frees us from her suffering. Once dressed in her last traveling outfit, she is taken down to the mortuary, where we join her in total sadness. We recall her last moments, each of us lost in thoughts, without knowing how to express our pain.

Then she was taken to the funeral home in Brie-Comte-Robert, where no one had the strength to visit her. My sister Zeu's words sum up exactly what her life has been like:

"She's over there, all alone in the big room, with no one to come and visit her." I imagine her alone in that cold room, waiting for a visitor who does not come... My nights are sleepless, and my days are hopeless.

On the day of the funeral, the five of us set out to bring her things, which we put in her coffin-ship. We put her makeup on; my mother is almost beautiful; she never shone with physical beauty but always tried to be a beautiful mother to all her siblings.

Her funeral took place during the week of July 14, 2012, in a room next to the one where we had mourned our father so much. Family and friends come for a final tribute in a dignified and humble atmosphere. We do the same rituals as for my father, but everything is calmer, more serene.

She outlived three members of her family. That is enough: she has the right to rest, after so much suffering.

We experienced the end of our travel with her.

Nowadays

On the cassette she left us, her voice trembles with fever and no longer has the strength to rise, but there are no reproaches, no regrets, only the loving words of a courageous mother: "Continue to live together and to love each other."

Laos is far away now. We have blended into the French population. By trying to push aside our origins in order to better integrate, we have lost our way. Our traditions and cultures are lost.

We are trying hard to keep our parents' advice alive: will we, like them, be able to put aside our individual desires to allow the family to continue to live together in harmony?

In front of the Bisséous Tower (Castres)

First time at sea

France

Table of main proper names

Transcription	Hmong
Mao :	Mos
Tou :	Tub
Guia :	Nkias
Tseu :	Ntxawg
Choua :	Suav
Pheng :	Phiab
Blia :	Npliaj
Zeu :	Ntxawm
Nadia :	Dawb
Kou :	Txooj
Zo :	Ntzov
May :	Maiv
Yen :	Yeeb
Xang :	Xab
Tcha :	Tsab
Heu :	Hawj
Lis :	Lis
Vang :	Vaj
Vang Pao :	Vaj pov
Blia Tchong :	Npliaj Tsooj
Txi Tchou :	Txiv Tsu
Yaeu Noa :	Yawg Nom
Tcha Yia :	Tsav Yias
Gnay-Vang :	Nchaiv Vaj
Gua-Ning :	Nkaj Neeb
Blia Txia :	Npliaj Txiam
Say Txong :	Xaiv Txoov

Table of main cities in Laos

Transcription	Hmong
Paksé :	Phaj Kheb
Phao-Khao :	Phoj Kaom
Long-Cheng :	Looj Ceeb
Té-Niou-Crou :	Teb Nyuj Qus
Phu-Mou :	Phwv Mus
Hin Heu :	Heev heus
Pa-Ning :	Phaj Neeb
Pu-Nieu :	Phwv Nyaws
Na-Nyos :	Nas Nyos
Pa-Son :	Paj Xoom
Vinaï :	Vib Nai
Na-Sou :	Nas Xus

WHAT MORE...

A little history

Hmong story of Laos begins in Yunan, China, in the early 20th century. Constantly in conflict with the Chinese government, which tried to sedentarize this nomadic people who called themselves "free" men (without submission to a government), some Hmong migrated to southern Asia and settled in Thailand, Vietnam, Laos...

Great farmers, they cultivated rice and corn for their own consumption, then began growing opium to sell to neighboring and Western countries, including colonial France.

During the Indochina War, they paid a heavy price in human losses, fighting alongside the French against Vietnam (March 13-May 7, 1954: Battle of Dien Bien Phu). During the Vietnam War (1959-1975), the Americans set up an air base in Long-Cheng Province and enlisted men and children to wage war against communism. In Laos, the Hmong had to fight against other Hmong, siding with the Pathet-Lao, the Laotian Communist Party, born under the inspiration of the Viet-Minh.

In 1975, there were about 30,000 Hmong living in the province, fed by the American government, which regularly dropped bags of food onto the military base.

After more than 22 years of conflict, the Americans withdrew and abandoned Laos and its Hmong "allies". Hunted for treason by their own brothers, the Hmong who had fought alongside the Westerners had to flee or risk being shot.

Those Hmong who were not lucky enough to be picked up by the repatriation helicopters decided to flee into the forest, while others preferred to stay and continue cultivating their fields. Those who reach Thailand are herded into refugee camps with other ethnic minorities forced to flee for fear of communist repression: the Phai, the Thin, the Yao, the Khmou, the Mlabri...

The international community reacts by organizing the reception of refugees. France and the United States are the primary host countries (1,000 refugees per month).

On December 29, 2009, Laos and Thailand signed an agreement to repatriate the Hmong to Laos. The camps were dismantled.

Today, a few thousand Hmong still live in the forest.

BETWEEN CUSTOMS, TRADITIONS, AND CULTS

Customs, traditions, and worship differ slightly depending on the clan to which each Hmong belongs. There are the White Hmong, who make up the majority of the ethnic group, followed by the Green Hmong and the Hmong with "striped" sleeves.

Everyone speaks the same dialect with a slight difference in pronunciation. The following information concerns mainly the White Hmong.

To be born

In the Hmong countryside, even when pregnant, the woman works all the time until the child is born, which she delivers with a midwife at home. Afterward, she must not leave her baby's side for a month, during which she feeds on freshly killed chicken broth; she must also cover her head, hands, and feet and dress warmly.

For one month, she is not allowed to visit her family. It comes from the animist belief that "the spirits of her husband's clan" should not meet the "spirits of her birth family's clan," as if the innocence of the newborn opened the door to the spirits of the afterlife...

After a month, a "*khi tes*[56]" ceremony is organized to formalize the union within the community: family and friends are invited to share a cheerful meal.

---

56 *Khi tes*: it is a ceremony in which a cotton thread is tied on the wrist for good luck. It's a ceremony for all the right occasions: birth, wedding...

Being a boy

In a patriarchal community, the man is responsible for the reputation of the entire family and clan.

Each clan can include thousands of individuals who do not necessarily know each other. Marriage within the same clan is strictly forbidden: this act is worse than any crime, as it is considered incestuous.

An old Hmong legend tells that a long time ago, the Earth experienced a flood that drowned all men. Only one brother and one sister remained. They went to see the soothsayer, the "shao", who told them to mate so that the human race could be reborn. They obeyed, but the child born of this union had no head or limbs and looked like a squash. "Shao" told them to cut the squash into small pieces and scatter them: one piece to the north, another to the south, a third to the east, another near a riverbank, and so on... The next day, they were surprised to see a couple crouching beside a crackling fire at each place where they had left a piece of their baby. Each couple formed a clan: the Ly Clan, the Xiong Clan, the Yang Clan, the Moua Clan, the Lor Clan, the Heu Clan...

The weight of the lineage is such that every male must preserve traditions at all costs in order to pass this heritage on to the youngest son. Polygamy is commonly practiced and is all the more legitimate if the first wife does not bear a son. A man can have several wives to ensure his descendants.

It is thanks to the clan and the family that a man can establish his reputation and be well perceived by the rest of the community: a man who has few brothers, cousins, uncles, or none at all, sees his existence reduced to little consideration. Therefore, as disputes are settled between men, those with few families to represent them can only timidly ask for help from other clans, which, one thing leading to another, turn out to be distant relatives.

The Hmong are very supportive of one another.

Being a girl

Girls are educated to become good future wives and must leave the family home of birth. In the countryside, they often have no access to schooling, which is considered a waste of time and a lost investment for the family of birth.

At a very young age, they work from morning to night, all year round, until they reach marriageable age, sometimes at twelve or thirteen. They are not allowed to refuse the husband chosen for them by their parents.

Their marriage is sometimes like a sale since the groom's parents must pay a dowry, which is measured in kilos of gold and silver ingots.

Once married, they lose their very existence, right down to their first and last names. In fact, they are called by their husband's first name.

Women's lives are very difficult. They contribute a great deal to household chores by helping their mothers, and when they marry, they must be capable of running the family home for their husbands. Contraception is non-existent, and women are often pregnant from one year to the next.

Getting married

Before taking a wife, the boy must inform his parents of the origin of his intended. It is followed by a thorough investigation into each other's background by both parties. It is advisable to marry close relatives; in some cases, the bride and groom are first cousins. But above all, you must not be part of the same clan: even unrelated cousins necessarily have an origin from the same line, however distant it may be.

Once inquiries have been made, confirming that the bride and groom are not related and are from good families, the groom "kidnaps" the girl. If the two future spouses agree on this kidnapping, the girl quietly follows the boy. If the girl has no interest in the boy, she is forcibly abducted and has no choice but to marry him to preserve her parents' honor.

The boy's parents send a messenger to inform the girl's parents that they intend to come and ask for her hand in marriage. A date is set. Three days later, the bride and groom travel to the bride's home, accompanied by several trusted men appointed by the parents to represent them. These include the negotiator and his substitutes, the best man and maid of honor, and the cooks who will prepare a meal for the bride's family.

Negotiations can last several days, at the end of which the bride and groom and their attendants must return home with the bride. The bride's family must prepare a meal for the return journey. From this moment on, the girl leaves her birth family for good, to live a life totally dedicated to her husband and in-laws. The objects of the negotiation are scrupulously notified to all the witness-representatives of both parties who, in the event of future disputes, are called upon to defend one or the other party.

The girl's parents often demand a fairly substantial dowry, which sometimes puts off young suitors who do not have the money.

Healing

The Hmong are animists. Between beliefs and superstitions, the country is filled with ghosts, wandering souls, and a troubled spirit that can be malevolent. If it enters a house, it might want to stay and torment its occupants.

Any illness or unexplained behavior is considered the work of spirits. It is then necessary to seek the help of the shaman. The latter possesses the key that allows him to communicate with the spirits. He takes his gong, bells, and buffalo horns to the sick person's house. After a preliminary dance that can last for hours, he enters a trance and speaks a language unknown to all: the language of the spirits. He invokes them and asks them the object of their anger. Then, he attempts a dialogue to negotiate the healing of the sick person and the appeasement of his angry spirit.

This healing is achieved in exchange for a sacrifice. One can imagine all kinds of possible sacrifices: the more complex the disease is to cure, the greater the reward (chicken, pig, cow...).

The gift of shamanism is passed down from generation to generation. Sometimes several members of the same family are entrusted with this mission within the same generation or from one generation to the next. However, each family practices the ritual differently.

One does not become a shaman by one's own will. The spirits impose themselves on the person through whom they wish to convey their wishes, and that person cannot resist: they must respond favorably to their requests under penalty of all kinds of torture and abuse (illness, insomnia, irrational behavior). And this can last for a certain time, months, or even years.

There are several ways to practice shamanism:

1. Shamanism known as "neeb cag" or "neeb txwb zeej": this is a gift of shamanism passed down from generation to generation, the purpose of which is to heal.
2. Shamanism known as "neeb saub": a diviner is called upon to relieve physical or spiritual ailments.
3. Shamanism known as "poj qhi": in front of a fire, the shaman uses a spoon as a key to open the door to the afterlife and meet the spirits.

Few Hmong understand the complete ritual of a shamanism session.

I recommend reading the book by Dr. Jean-Pierre Willem, a doctor without borders who treated the refugees of Nam-Yao in 1977 (pages 64-65: Les naufragés de la liberté – available only in digital format, in French). He mentions 16 levels that the shaman must climb in order to reach heaven to meet the good spirits and ask for their favor on behalf of the sick person.

Hmong Ceremonies: Khi tes and Hu Plig

These are essential steps in the life of a Hmong. The Khi tes ceremony consists of tying a thread around the wrist of the person in whose honor the ceremony is being offered. Each time a knot is tied, the tyer must make a vow of goodwill.

This ceremony is performed on any celebratory occasion: birth, marriage, name change, hu plig, etc. While it is more cultural in nature, the hu plig ceremony has an aspect linked to animist beliefs. Indeed, this second ceremony involves calling upon the spirits to heal and appease the person's soul. It is always accompanied by an animal sacrifice. One cannot be performed without the other, but the converted no longer practice the hu plig ceremony, which is contrary to their new religion.

Becoming a Man

When a man is married and reaches a certain age of "maturity," he changes his first name. It often happens at the age of forty and when he becomes a father.

It is said that he takes an "old man" name. This new name is often composed of his first name and a particle that gives him a certain notoriety.

Sometimes, he changes his first name completely. From then on, he is recognized within his clan by his new name. There are no rites of passage, as in some animist communities, only a meal prepared in his honor by his parents who choose this new name for him. Family and friends are invited to the meal, preceded by a "khi tes" ceremony that formalizes this appointment in the eyes of the entire community.

Embroidery

Embroidery is a women's business. The clothes are sewn by women, who pass this knowledge on to their daughters from a very young age. Whenever they have free time, they embroider sleeves, aprons, and shirt trims, which are then sewn onto the outfits that make up the festive costumes for the end of the year. It takes almost a whole year to make a costume. Each province has its own costume; there may be around twenty.

The more colorful and embroidered with geometric figures, the more it signifies wealth.

Once a year, there is a New Year's celebration, an opportunity for young people to meet and find their life partner.

It is said that in ancient times, the Hmong's geometric and colorful patterns represented a form of writing. During a war, two brothers attempted to escape with their precious literary treasures embroidered on fabrics but were caught by their enemies while crossing a river. They were killed, and their bodies ended up at the bottom of the river with Hmong writing. Truth or legend? There are no written records to confirm or deny this story……

New Year

It is one of the rare festive moments for the Hmong. The New Year is celebrated over several days. It is the time to bring out clothes embroidered with colorful threads and silver necklaces. As mentioned several times, young people take advantage of this time to court each other in song duels, the "kwv txhiaj," which are excelled by all. These traditional Hmong songs are without music. They are related to the Portuguese "Fado." They are songs of immediate inspiration without preparation or written notes. They are inspired by daily life and are untranslatable; only trained ears understand their meaning. During the New Year Festival, young people play the game of "ball throwing" to court each other. The one who does not catch the ball must sing a song to the other to express their feelings. The other must respond in song. The melody is slow and moves the listener to the deepest depths. These "kwv txhiaj" are sung on all occasions: they are songs of separation, mourning, loneliness, nostalgia...

The songs we know in the West appeared around 1975. The song "Xyoo 75" encapsulates the difficult choice of those who decided to leave everything behind to save their lives, a year that will remain etched in the collective memory.

The year 1975

In May 1975
Our country went to war
We had to leave our homes, our fields, and our animals
Our hearts were torn as we abandoned our farms
It was for real, and our faces darkened
Amidst the hills,
we turned our gaze one last time
We heard the cries of our panicked animals
Our tears flowed endlessly, but we could confide in no one...
Our fathers carried the little ones while our mothers followed behind
The youngest clung to their fathers' necks
The babies were tied to their mothers' bellies
Because of the war, we are without a homeland or a country
We are like animals without honor
Would there ever be a day when we would finally return to our country?

Writing

Hmong culture was traditionally and entirely oral. Young people learned the customs and traditions of their clan from their elders through stories, songs, and recitations.

The Hmong writing system was codified in 1953 through the joint work of French priest Yves Bertrais, a Protestant pastor named Roff, an American missionary, and a linguistic specialist. This script, called "Hmong RPA Writing" (Romanized Popular Alphabet), uses the Latin alphabet. However, there are pronunciation differences between the White Hmong and the Green Hmong, similar to accents. It gradually became universal for all Hmong, against the wishes of the Laotian government, which wanted all ethnic groups in the territory to use Laotian characters. Hmong writing has, therefore, been directly linked to the history of evangelization. Although the Hmong diaspora often used cassettes to send news, the Hmong RPA script enabled the sending of letters to thousands of emigrants. It contributed to the survival of the Hmong language and culture.

Among the Hmong

The Hmong consider themselves one big family. As they practice the cult of the Elders, they visualize their place in the family so that they can name other members accordingly. When addressing an uncle or aunt, they use a different term depending on whether they are a boy or a girl.

Si on est :	*Grande sœur*	*Petite sœur*
Fille	Niam laus	Niam hluas
Garçon	Muam hlob	Muam yau

Si on est :	*Grand frère*	*Petit frère*
Fille	Nus hlob	Nus yau
Garçon	Tij laug hlob	Kwv yau

Once married, parents are addressed differently, positioning themselves on the children's side:

- "niam tais, yawm txiv": maternal grandmother, maternal grandfather,
- "niam pog, txiv yawg": paternal grandmother, paternal grandfather.

These are simple examples. Elders should teach young people these names, which are considered signs of respect for their elders.

Dying

Death is omnipresent in the life of a Hmong. But, contradictorily, one never truly dies. Every Hmong believes in reincarnation, life after death, and continuity in everyday life (marked by the cult of the Elders). Therefore, funeral ceremonies are burdensome and expensive for the family of the deceased. Indeed, they can last up to a week (night and day), depending on the importance of the deceased. They are generally held in the deceased's home, where they lie with their head facing east. In France, the ceremony takes place over a weekend.

Locals flock there, and a formal ritual is formalized by experts appointed for the occasion. This ritual concludes with the soul of the deceased being sent to the place where their ancestors continue to live, waiting for them and welcoming them among them.

Therefore, they must not take the wrong path. The family prepares branches of paper, symbols of money, to allow him to pay for his journey, to feed himself, and especially to pay the entrance fee for his passage to the afterlife.

Songs are sung to ward off evil spirits from his path because, just like a newborn, he knows nothing of the life of spirits and must not be led astray to forbidden places or get lost between Earth and Heaven. It is said that a Hmong has three spirits: one goes to join his ancestors, one is reborn, and the third continues his life among the living... It is the essence of his descendants.

Today, many Hmong have converted to Catholicism or Protestantism, but this way of paying tribute to the deceased remains alive. There is still a vigil throughout the weekend. Among Catholic converts, it is the priest who formalizes the steps of sending the soul to Heaven and its resurrection.

Books references

Only in French

1. *Les naufragés de la liberté. Le dernier exode des Méos* – Dr Jean-Pierre Willem - SOS Editions (1980). N'existe que sous format numérique.

2. *La langue Hmong* – Barbara Niederer (article internet).

3. *Allons faire le tour du Ciel et de la Terre. Le chamanisme des Hmong vu dans les textes* – Jean Mottin (1981).

4. *Les Hmong du Laos en France* – Jean-Pierre Hassoun (Ed. PUF).

5. *Les Hmong de la Péninsule indochinoise* – Christian Culas et Jean Michaud (article internet).

6. Isabelle Alleton, " *Les Hmong aux confins de la Chine et du Viêtnam: la révolte du " Fou "* (1918-1922) ", in *L'histoire de l'Asie du Sud-Est. Révoltes, réformes, révolutions*, (éd.) Pierre Rocheux, Lille, Presses universitaires de Lille, 1981, p. 31-46.

7. *Ne me lâche pas la main* - Cathou Quivy (Ed. Stellamaris).

Special thanks

*Thanks to my family
for agreeing to relive our story by publishing it here.
Thanks to my nieces and nephews
for their support and advice.
Thanks to my aunts and uncles
for sharing their stories with me.
Thanks to my daughters and my husband
who supported me during the writing of this book.
Thanks to my parents
for their posthumous testimonies and for all they gave us: love,
hope, unity and respect for life.*

*Thanks to Brigitte L.
without whom this project would never have begun.*

*Special thanks to Patricia and her husband,
and Xoblaim who translate with passion this book.*

Without your help, it could not be printed.

© 2025 Maiv Lis
Publisher : BoD · Books on Demand,
31 avenue Saint-Rémy, 57600 Forbach, bod@bod.fr
Printer : Libri Plureos GmbH,
Friedensallee 273, 22763 Hamburg (Allemagne)
ISBN : 978-2-3225-9518-1
Dépôt légal : Avril 2025